From the Back of the Line

From the Back of the Line

The Views of A Teenager From the 1960s Civil Rights Movement

Rev. Dr. Gloria Ward Wright

Library of Congress Control Number:		2006905892
ISBN 10:	Hardcover	1-4257-2119-2
	Softcover	1-4257-2118-4
ISBN 13:	Hardcover	978-1-4257-2119-0
	Softcover	978-1-4257-2118-3

This book was printed in the United States of America.

To order additional copies of this book, contact:
Xlibris Corporation
1-888-795-4274
www.Xlibris.com
Orders@Xlibris.com
28147

CONTENTS

Preface by William Nelson Martin 9

Foreword by Kay Smith Pedrotti 11

Prologue 15

1   A Jail Bird Can't Fly 17

2   Moving Through the Line: My Journey 28

3   Headquarters at My Mt. Zion 39

4   Cheerleader for Justice 44

5   Life Lessons 57

6   Gloria and Kay: Forgiveness and Friendship 69

7   Response to Dr. Martin Luther King, Jr.'s Speech Forty-three Years Later 73

8   Where Have All The Leaders Gone? 81

9   Preordained to be Ordained 88

10 The Way I See It: Commentary on the Past, the Present, and the Future 100

Epilogue 119

Appendix 121

The Civil Rights Act of 1964 131

Suggested Reading 133

Statements of Endorsement: *From the Back of the Line* 135

Acknowledgments 143

"Whether you turn to the right or to the left, your ears will hear a voice behind you, saying, "This is the way; walk in it."

Isaiah 30:21 (NIV)

Byron Ward Wright

DEDICATION

To my son, Byron Ward Wright. I offer you my mantle.
And to the sons and daughters of those who marched for freedom
with me at the back of the line.

*Walk into your destiny, for your future is bright because
you are blessed and highly favored of the Lord.*

PREFACE

The nature of the civil rights movement as we knew it from the 1950s through the 1980s has changed so dramatically that children and young adults today have difficulty understanding and relating to it. As a whole, those of us who were involved during those years have not done all we should to transmit the knowledge, wisdom, and emotion to younger generations.

From the Back of the Line is an attempt to rectify that omission and advance the new dialogue that is needed today. We can only hope that the glow from the flame will attract and enlighten many young minds and will remind the original warriors not to let their torches die out before they are passed on to the warriors of today and tomorrow. Congratulations to Reverend Gloria Ward Wright, a great keeper and transmitter of the flame through her work as teacher, pastor, author, and engaging human being, for writing *From the Back of the Line*. Let each of us make a commitment to provide at least a spoonful of fuel for the flame.

As a result of continuing adherence to the ideals of leaders like the Reverend Martin Luther King, Jr., the movement and its aftermath have been transformative—even to the extent of changing attitudes of many who have been opponents of advancements by African-Americans. Illustrative of this transformation is the story of journalist Kay Smith Pedrotti who, as a white teenager growing up in Albany, Georgia, could not accept the fact that blacks "wouldn't stay in their place." She underwent dramatic transformation, as noted in her Foreword to *From the Back of the Line* and in Chapter 6.

The transformation is evident in the life of the author and visionary, Gloria Ward Wright, who also had a dream that one day the youth of this country and the world would learn of the sacrifices of their ancestors, leaders who boldly stepped out on faith in the belief that we, African-Americans, will not accept second-class citizenship.

This autobiographical and inspirational book will give readers another perspective of the civil rights movement in the United States of America, "the land of the free and the home of the brave." This is the perspective of those who marched for freedom from the back of the line—the youth. Were it not for young people, there would not have been a line at all. Because the youth followed those who were at the front of the line, great strides were made. The youth at the back of the line, however, did grow up. Where are they today? Are they ready to stand tall at the front of the line, to lead others to a better tomorrow?

—William Nelson Martin,
Attorney-at-Law and former
State Senator, North Carolina

FOREWORD

Rev. Dr. Gloria Ward Wright invites Mrs. Kay Smith Pedrotti to her church to speak
The two had met for the first time after thirty-five years of silence and racial tension.

To understand the impact that Gloria Ward Wright has had on my life—and is about to have on yours—I need to take you from the back of that long, liberating line to the front of the bus and to the dining room, not the kitchen, of a restaurant in Albany, Georgia.

In that all-white restaurant, in the summer of 1962, an Associated Press reporter asked me to provide my views for an article he was writing about civil rights demonstrations in my hometown and throughout the South. I had just graduated from all-white Albany High School. The reporter would contrast my segregationist feelings with those of Gloria Ward, a student at all-black Monroe High School, who was marching for freedom. Gloria followed the illustrious and brought her own courage with her. I reviled them and denied my cowardice.

The story ran in newspapers across the country. We both survived that nationwide exposure. (I got a lot of hate mail.) I later had a redemption-conversion experience. I recovered from racism. But it was thirty-five years later that Gloria and I found each other, forgave (Both of us did manage to forgive me.), and reconciled. What I want to say to readers on these pages is that Gloria will impact your life in the most wonderful of ways even if you never meet her, even if you never do anything connected with her except read this book.

She has made me see the many times when God was leading me to become a different person, even as I was growing up under the rigid strictures of the white rules for interaction with "Negroes." (Usually called by another name, but because we had "manners," my sister and I would usually say "colored people.")

There was a time when I cried for all of us white and black folks who missed the wonderful things we could have meant to each other, learned from each other, done for each other. That occurred when I attended the funeral of the mother of an African-American friend, Dyan Matthews. I did not know Dyan's mother, but I loved and respected Dyan and wanted to show her I cared. I did more caring than I ever thought I would.

Several pews in front of me in the small chapel, I recognized the hair of Mary Lizzie Polite, parted in the middle, two big braids starting at the part and meeting in the back like a crown of glory, of thorns. I could feel Mary Lizzie's arms around me as a child and hear her chuckle while she ironed in our middle bedroom. My mother was appalled when I asked Mary Lizzie her last name and then called her "Miz Polite." That was the first glimmer of my future.

When I saw that long-forgotten hairdo at Dyan's mother's funeral—a place one can cry—my tears were my guilt, my sadness, my painful truth. The childish trick of calling that beloved woman, who left her own family to take care of us, by her last name—I did not know then that it was not allowed. But I insisted on doing it, because I thought all older folks should be Miz or Mister Somebody or something respectful. Only God could have told me that. Thank you, Mrs. Mary Lizzie Polite. I know you are at the front of the line, wherever you are.

Many more people in my life have pointed the way to wholeness, but the four who had the greatest effect on me, before Gloria in 1997, were Cynthia Wesley, Addie Mae Collins, Carole Robertson, and Denise McNair. I never met them, but I knew when they died, along with the rest of the country. They died in the Sixteenth Street Baptist Church bombing in Birmingham, Alabama, September 15, 1963. They were studying a Sunday school lesson called "The Love That Forgives" when that terrible terrorist act took them from their families.

One was only eleven years old. The others fourteen, the same age as my little sister. Why had children been killed? I had been told that nobody got hurt in violent white responses to civil rights struggles, that the tactics were to "scare" the black people into "behaving themselves." My mind could not hold that horror of imagining my sister's or any fourteen-year-old's body mangled by a bomb IN CHURCH and knowing that those four were somebody's sisters, daughters, grandchildren. And so I began truly to pray and study and think for myself. By the fall of 1964, I left Albany a changed person.

It may seem incredible that, as a reporter, I could not find Gloria and seek her forgiveness for thirty-five years. But the truth is, as an adult, I knew no black people in Albany. I had a life, a career, children, all the busy things. But I never stopped thinking about Gloria. Unlike many white people who have moved beyond their prejudice and bigotry, I could put a name on somebody I had hurt.

We have only God to credit and thank that we did find each other, and that we have begun the process of telling our stories to new generations. I look at young white people and want to ask, "Don't you know that sitting next to a black person in school doesn't make you less a racist? Look inside and find the truth." And I look at black teenagers and want to say, "You are worth so much more than anyone can believe, even yourself. Look inside and learn to respect who you are and who you come from." Start with this book.

Now, my beloved friend follows her Lord and stands at the "front" when she preaches. The back of the line, the cold concrete floors of the jails, the swelling songs of the march—these things helped to shape her into the vessel that overflows with love. I've been splashed again and again. Thank you, Mrs. (Dr.!) Gloria Ward Wright.

—Kay Smith Pedrotti
Jonesboro, Georgia

PROLOGUE

D r. Martin Luther King, Jr., inspired me as a youth of sixteen. I saw and felt what it was like to be discriminated against. Children today don't know this, and that's why it's so important to teach it. Today is a different era, a different time. We need to deal with our children and youth in another way. They need to know their history, but they don't need to look in the rearview mirror all the time. Current civil rights leaders are aging and need someone to step into their places. We can't keep living just on Dr. King's dream. We, too, have dreams, and they ought to be offsprings of his dream. We are living in some perilous times. We have to have some youth who are going to step up to the plate ready to bat for our future, young people who may start out at the back of the line but are ready to move to the front. Education is the key.

This book is a clarion call—a wake up call for the youth of this world, especially African-Americans. It is time for all our young people to take their rightful places as leaders as African-Americans, Africans, Native Americans, Asian Americans, Hispanics, Latinos, Jews, and Gentiles. There is strength in numbers. The time has come for those of us who were at the back of the line in the civil rights movement to step up to the front of the line and take our positions of responsible leadership. Why? Because others at the back of the line are ready to follow successful leaders. We must lead the way. We must teach our youth how to lead. We must teach them our history, teach them about our struggles and about our accomplishments. And our youth must be open and receptive in order to benefit from the wisdom of those who have paved the way.

There are so many bright and gifted youth who, with the wisdom of their elders, can bring about very positive change in our society. They must, however, use the road maps that our leaders have left as a great legacy.

It is time to work together and walk together "for the sake of others." If the leaders who were and are at the front of the line do not pass the mantle, then the youth must take up a new mantle and march on to victory. They need our input; they need to know our history. We who know the way must lead the way. We cannot afford to get weary, we cannot afford to be timid, we cannot afford to become violent, but we must, respectfully keep moving for time waits for no one.

America is truly my home, where we, African-Americans, fought for our rights as a proud people who helped to build this country "from sea to shining sea." We must maintain a free world where generations and generations yet unborn must live harmoniously in a society that should demand to be protected from the darts of racism, discrimination, and violence. We must continue in our quest to live in peace and harmony.

—Rev. Gloria Ward Wright

1

A Jail Bird Can't Fly

"Let brotherly love continue. Be not forgetful to entertain strangers: for thereby some have entertained angels unawares." . . . Hebrews 13:1-2 (KJV)

My fourth arrest wasn't supposed to happen. I hadn't dressed for the occasion. I was wearing high-heeled shoes because I had just attended the funeral of a young man who had been shot by police. I was sixteen years old that early spring of 1962.

I showed up at the march simply to support my classmates from Monroe High School. I went to the back of the line where I would be out of the fray because my mother had warned me that my luck might run out one day. I had survived the first three arrests with the usual discomfort that jail brings. I might not be so fortunate another time around.

I stood there in spiritual solidarity with hundreds of people singing and standing steadfast for justice. I was not expecting an invitation that would test my commitment to the movement.

Suddenly a police officer barked at me, "Are you with them?"

Bloodshot eyes confronted me. His voice was full of hatred and venom. The rage in me sprang forth, and I defiantly answered, "Yes, I'm in this line."

It seemed like a spur of the moment decision on the surface. But not really. After all, I had been in the back of the line for many other marches. In my teenage quest to change the world, it had become a comfortable spot for me. Even though I would be criticized by a white teenager, Kay Smith, in a front-page newspaper story for being a "fool" and a "pawn" of the movement, I knew I was doing something that mattered—marching for equal civil rights in the small town of Albany in southwest Georgia, marching to affirm and elevate the humanity of my people. I was willing to put my life on the line in exchange for justice that would later transcend my reality and that of my parents, my six siblings, my teachers, my church, and my community. We had no idea that what we were doing—which would become known as the

Albany Movement—would serve as a model to liberate oppressed people all around the world.

Leaders of the Albany Movement wanted as many people as possible to participate in nonviolent mass demonstrations and marches against segregation. We came from all over the city—young, old, short, tall, black, red. Other demonstrators joined us from around the country as the Albany Movement grew. The goal was to voice our demands—to desegregate public facilities, schools, movie theaters, etc. When our demands were not met, the plan was to fill up the jails. Of course, the marches were designed to get us arrested. Each time, the charges were basically the same: parading without a permit, obstruction of justice, and refusing to disperse.

Before every march, movement leaders held mass meetings. Rev. Samuel Wells and Rev. Charles Sherrod instructed us to kneel and pray while we were placed under arrest. We were instructed not to walk but to make the police carry us. Sometimes that worked. Other times, after they grew tired of carrying so many marchers, the police resorted to pushing us and trying to force us to walk. This was to make their jobs easier. At times we were pushed around, but we remembered to remain nonviolent and not to provoke the police.

While we were being arrested, we could see Mr. A.C. Searles, the editor and owner of the only black newspaper at that time, *The Southwest Georgian*, walking up and down the sidewalk with a camera hanging from his shoulder and a notepad in his hand. Mr. Searles' newspaper kept us informed about the black community in general and especially about the Albany Movement. We could not rely on the white owned paper, the *Albany Herald,* to report fully and accurately about the African-American community at that time.

Mr. Benjamin Cochran of Cochran Studio also took pictures for posterity. Some of the same pictures taken by Mr. Cochran are included in this book to help tell the story. Although Mr. Cochran is deceased, his photography studio still carries his name and the business still flourishes with new owner and photographer, A.E. Jenkins. Someone once said that a picture speaks a thousand words. I do agree because, as I look at some of the pictures that were taken during the Albany Movement, many things that I had forgotten come to mind because of those pictures.

Off to a Cell

Two burly police officers picked me up by my arms to carry me off to "Freedom Alley," our name for the Albany City Jail's holding area, a narrow, dinky walkway that doubled as a storage space for stolen bicycles and other goods. After my earlier arrests, I had sat on the concrete floor and waited to be booked. By my fourth arrest, I knew the routine. I was not afraid. Yet the number of buses and the paddy wagon waiting nearby were unusual. Dr. William G. Anderson, the President of the Albany Movement, and Rev. Dr. Martin Luther King, Jr., who was in Albany to support us, hadn't counted on their presence. Neither had I.

Thirteen girls and I were forced into a paddy wagon. We expected to be transported to the Albany City Jail. But this time Police Chief Laurie Pritchett had a surprise for us. The paddy wagon kept going. Still, I remained calm. Some girls started crying. We were traveling into unknown territory at the mercy of people who had already clearly demonstrated their capacity for cruelty. We eased our anxiety by singing freedom songs. Finally our journey ended at Camilla, Georgia, about twenty-five miles southeast of Albany. No one knew what to expect next.

After my earlier arrests, we weren't taken out of town. Instead we went to the Albany (Dougherty County) City Jail where men and boys were held on the second level, women and girls on the first level. The cells were so crowded that we had to stand most of the time, but we could at least talk through the windows to people who had gathered outside. One of the worst things was the toilet—which was not enclosed so whenever one of us had to use it, other girls created a human shield so that the men, and especially the white jailers, couldn't get the pleasure of subjecting us to more humiliation.

Mitchell County Jail in Camilla was a different story. We were placed in a roach-infested fifteen-by-thirty foot room with four bunk beds. The filthy blue and gray striped mattresses reeked with foul odors. The cell had a shower, but it was filled with trash, milk cartons, discarded food, and an assortment of things we couldn't decipher.

Our meals were brought systematically every morning. Grits and grease with white bread, or "light bread," as we called it. It was Sunbeam bread with a white blonde girl's picture on the package. This was my favorite bread at home, so smooth and soft and certainly more palatable than grits and grease. For dinner we had overcooked rice with just enough tomato sauce to turn it pink, and more Sunbeam bread. We ate the bread and balled up the rice and threw it at each other, just for fun. Anything to pass the time. We also prayed and sang freedom songs. Fourteen girls in one jail cell, far away from home, facing an uncertain future.

On the second day at Camilla, we formed a circle and prayed. I prayed for food other than dreadful greasy grits and pink rice. "Lord, please send us some decent food to eat." Later that afternoon, a miracle happened!

A jailer came to our cell and yelled, "Is there a Gloria Ward in there?"

Some of the girls, showing their lack of maturity, crooned, "Oooh, Gloria. They gonna get you." Whatever that meant.

Still, I answered, "Yes, Sir!" I knew how to stay in good graces with the jailer.

"I have a package for you," he said. I was clueless. Who would be sending me a package in Camilla? The other girls were just as curious but fearful, too. They were afraid that the package could be a bomb. It did occur to me that we could be given something to kill us or make us ill.

The jailer slowly pushed the package through the small opening in the cell's iron door. My captive audience stared as I carefully opened the brown paper bag. To my surprise, there was food! Wrapped in wax paper and foil were four pieces of fried chicken, collard greens, macaroni and cheese, candied yams, cornbread, and a big mason jar of iced tea! The aroma of these southern delicacies bathed the jail cell with the sweetness of home.

But who had sent me food? Then a light bulb went off in my head. My oldest sister Barbara's in-laws owned a funeral home, Jester's Mortuary, in Camilla. I was sure they had sent the food. They were very prominent people in Camilla and probably the only ones the sheriff would have allowed to do this kind deed.

The girls were breathless. They swamped me like bees to a honeycomb. I cried out, "Thank you Jesus! There is a God!

"Okay, everybody, listen up," I announced. "I love all of you, and I know you are hungry, but the chicken leg and the tea are mine. You will have to fight it out for the rest!"

In an instant, I learned how many times three pieces of chicken could be divided among thirteen girls. And we learned two important lessons: First, ask and you shall receive, if you believe. I believed that my prayer would be answered. However, I had no idea that my prayer would be answered that soon with that kind of food. Second, we can understand how Jesus fed 5,000 with the little boy's lunch of two fish and five loaves of bread.

Passing Time in Jail

Jail is a stabilizer, even when you're sixteen. Time ceases to be important, and a watch is useless. Without fail, whenever somebody asked, "What time is it?" the response was a round of laughter because it really didn't matter. Or someone replied, "What time is it? Why? Do you have some place to go? Do you have an appointment? Need to catch the soaps?" There was nothing to do but wait. We could not bathe or brush our teeth. Days went by like the agonizing drip of water from a faucet.

One day I peered out the cell window and caught a glimpse of downtown Camilla. I also noticed black men wearing white jump suits with a blue stripe down the side of the pant leg. I later learned that these men were jail trustees who were permitted to perform duties out among the general public. We saw them walking outside the gate and returning with packages from the store.

We wanted items from the store, too, so on the third day of our residency at the Mitchell County Jail, we started screaming to the trustees below to ask for their help. We held on to the bars of the cell as we tried to communicate with them.

I was craving milk. I had a few dollars taped to the inside of my belt. We took the two dingy sheets that once were on those filthy mattresses and tied them together to make a ladder to let down the money and haul up the goods. Since I was the only one with money and we weren't supposed to have money on us, I decided that we needed to spend it while we had a chance. I ordered a small carton of sweet milk, which I really loved. The rest of the money was spent on cookies and bubble gum.

As soon as the trustee returned from the store, we lifted up our goodies. Suddenly the cell door opened, and we froze at the sight of a jailer and his German shepherd dog.

I am really afraid of most dogs. The dog headed straight toward me. The dog smelled the goodies or he sensed my fear. No matter the reason for his interest in me, I was not interested in him. I sat there frozen with my carton of milk and nervously said, "Hello, doggie." That dog was more frightening than the jailer. We had been told what to expect from jailers. We were told that they may rough us up, but don't provoke them and don't fight back. No one had told me how to respond to a canine. Thankfully the jailer was simply making his rounds with the dog, and they left quickly.

By the third day, our bodies were growing cold and our spirits were deteriorating. Still we continued to pray and sing freedom songs to keep our spirits up. The jailer would shout, "Cut out all that nigger noise." We lowered our volume, but that wasn't good enough. To keep us quiet, the jailers turned off the heat. We almost froze to death because we were sleeping on our coats on a concrete floor.

Even though the jailers used tactics to keep us from singing, those songs were in my heart. Singing the movement songs had become an integral part of my vernacular because we sang them whenever we protested. "Ain't Gonna Let Nobody Turn Me Around," "Oh Freedom," "This Little Light of Mine," "Oh Pritchett, Oh Kelly," "Everybody Say Amen," and "We Shall Overcome," were the songs we sang as we marched through the streets of downtown Albany.

While most sixteen-year-old girls around the country were singing along to Elvis or Ricky Nelson, I belted out a different repertoire, feeling the rush of adrenalin with each note. The songs gave me confidence and a feeling of exuberance. Freedom songs. Songs of the Albany Movement that we sang as we marched to what we referred to as "marching up to freedom land."

We sang the songs of the movement to give us hope, to encourage each other, and to alleviate any fear or anxiety. Most of the songs were sung to the tune of some of our Negro Spirituals. For instance, the freedom song, "Oh Pritchett, Oh Kelly" was sung in the tune to the old spiritual, "Rockin' in Jerusalem." The new lyrics spoke of the Police Chief Laurie Pritchett and the mayor of Albany at that time, Asa Kelly. "Oh Pritchett, Oh Kelly" was written by Janie Rambeau Culbreth and Bertha Gober who were students of Albany State College, now Albany State University.

When we weren't singing, we chanted slogans regarding our sought-after freedom. I knew and can remember all the original freedom singers except one, Charles Neblett. I knew Bernice Johnson Reagon who founded "Sweet Honey in The Rock," the Grammy Award-winning African-American female a cappella ensemble with deep musical roots in the sacred music of the black church. I knew her sister Mary Frances, now deceased, and their brother. I also knew Rutha Mae Harris, now a retired teacher, who has recently recorded her first CD. Her sister, McCree Harris, now deceased, was my homeroom teacher and French instructor at Monroe High School. Their brother Emory and I were friends. We marched together, were arrested together, and are still friends to this day.

When we marched, we knew we would be confronted by hatred and probably be arrested. A line of one particular freedom song, "Oh, Freedom," gave me courage . . . "and before I'll be a slave, I'll be buried in my grave and go home to my Lord and be free." As we demonstrated, we were serious about what we were doing for humanity and for posterity. White racists were serious about making trouble for us. They called us names and tried to intimidate us with rocks, sticks, and mean looks of hatred. They did not deter us, however. It was worth every mile that we walked and then some.

I was arrested and went to jail four times. Jail was no joke. No picnic. But I was never afraid. And thankfully, I was never hurt seriously. The police had so many people to carry to jail that they became frustrated and impatient. They called me a "niggra girl" and hurled other insults. We were pushed and slammed around like bags of trash. My body dropped onto the concrete floor more than once. But my bruises were nothing compared to others who were severely injured. Sheriff D.C. "Cull" Campbell beat the Albany Movement's attorney, C. B. King, over the head with a cane. He bled profusely as reporters watched.

The King family was prominent in Albany and made great contributions to the movement. Slater King was one of the presidents of the Albany Movement and Mrs. Marion King (now Mrs. Marion Jackson) made headlines when she was abused at the hands of the Camilla police and lost a child she was carrying.

Earlier Arrests

The first time I went to jail, we had marched to the courthouse where we were arrested, searched, and booked on several charges, including parading without a permit, creating a disturbance, failure to obey the command of an officer, and anything that they could use to "throw the book at us." I spent one night in jail with about eighteen girls. We had vowed to stay in jail no matter what. We sang and prayed. Outside our barred windows, we saw the people of Albany standing in the street. They shouted to us that we were seen on television. Parents and other people outside the jail window informed us that the news commentators had broadcast an appeal: "Please come and get your children."

Of course, we had promised to stay in jail. The idea was to fill the jails to capacity. Suddenly parents came to pick up their children. One by one, most of the girls went home. But five of us said that we were not going home. I felt that my parents were not going to come to get me. I felt this in my spirit. Since everybody was going home, it seemed senseless to me to remain alone in jail. I looked out at the crowd and saw Roosevelt, the cab driver who used to take my siblings and me to school. I screamed over the noise so that Roosevelt could hear me.

"If everyone leaves me here, I am going to need you to come and pick me up and take me home," I yelled. Eventually only one girl and myself were waiting to be picked up. I did not leave her, and she and I left about the same time.

The second time I was arrested, I remained in jail two nights. The third time, I was locked up for three nights. As the young people say, "You get my drift?" The fourth time that I was locked up, I was placed in the paddy wagon and taken away to Camilla, as I've already described.

Many youths were arrested fifteen to twenty times. Some were beaten and pistol-whipped. What a price so many paid for freedom. This is one of the reasons that I had to write this book. Adults have told stories regarding civil rights from their perspective. However, as a youth who marched "from the back of the line," I must tell the story from my perspective. I want today's youth to understand our seriousness and identify with teenagers of the 1950s and 1960s who demonstrated and fought against "legalized segregation" and abuse of citizens who paid taxes just as white people did. I want young people today to hear us as we demanded back then, "Why must we be discriminated against because we are people of color? Why must we drink water from a fountain that is not refrigerated when white people could drink cool water from refrigerated water fountains? Why must we shop in the stores for Christmas toys, spending just as much or more in department stores, but cannot use the rest rooms or eat at the lunch counters?"

For youth who never had to experience this kind of lifestyle, it is probably difficult to relate. I think that the whole idea about segregated society is so remote to some youth that it can be equated to how our generation related to slavery—we could not relate because we were not there. Nevertheless, we must read about what happened back in the day.

When I speak with young people today, I tell them: Understanding what happened with your parents and your grandparents should give you a new appreciation of your freedoms. Try to see this lesson about civil rights as a means of knowing just how far we have come. This will help you see how far we still have to go. Every generation must keep affirming what has been done. The new generation should never accept mediocrity. The struggle for our civil rights continues. We must never fall asleep and never allow blatant nor subtle acts of racism, of discrimination, or the evil of Jim Crowism to take over our society again. Just as some forms of slavery still exist, racism and discrimination are alive and well. Our youth must always keep their eyes open.

I agree with Rosa Parks, who wrote in her memoir, *Quiet Strength: The Faith, the Hope, and the Heart of a Woman Who Changed a Nation*, "One thing we need to do is tell young people about our struggles for civil rights. I think that they sometimes have difficulty separating fact from fiction when it comes to our history. It is important that they hear how things were and what some of us had to go through before them . . . What message would I have for young people today—of any race? Work hard, do not be discouraged, and in everything you do, try to make our country—and the world—a better place for us all. You are among my treasured friends and this country most treasured possession. You are our future."

Attorney C.B. King, a graduate of, both, Fisk University and Western Reserve University, was the main attorney for the Albany Movement. However, there were other attorneys who helped with legal matters of the movement and with the demonstrators' cases. A Loyola University Law School graduate Attorney Donald L. Hollowell, had worked with the well-publicized case involving Charlene Hunter and Hamilton Homes at the University of Georgia offered his expertise. This dynamite twosome, along with Attorney Constance Motley, made the legal decisions for the movement.

Hundreds of demonstrators, mainly students, marched the streets of Albany singing songs of freedom. Many were arrested and jailed. Some of the demonstrators were hurt physically and some were hurt emotionally by the hands of those in authority, especially in the smaller counties in southwest Georgia.

Leaders of the Southern Christian Leadership Conference leaving Albany City Hall. (L-R) Rev. Dr. Ralph David Abernathy, Rev. Wyatt T. Walker, Mrs. Coretta Scott King and Rev. Dr. Martin Luther King, Jr.

Freedom Alley was where the police would detain the demonstrators until they were booked. Many would kneel and pray until they were taken to their jail cells.

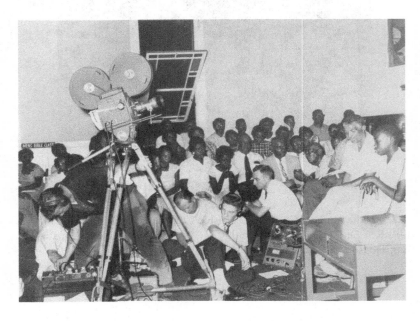

In Mt. Zion the media came from around the world to Albany to set up their cameras in anticipation of Dr. Martin Luther King, Jr.'s arrival.

Clergy came from all over the nation to offer their assistance to Albany and to Dr. Martin Luther King, Jr. Dr King addresses the clergy at Bethel AME Church, Albany, GA.

This is an example of what some of the jail cells looked like during the 1960s. The jail cells were filthy and did not meet federal standards?

2

Moving Through the Line: My Journey

"And we know that all things work together for good to them that love God, to them who are called according to his purpose." . . . . Romans 8:28 (KJV)

I began writing bits and pieces of this book forty-four years ago. At times, I had a strong desire to write. At other times, I experienced dry spells. I realized a few years ago that when you get older, you are made to recall many life experiences, but your memory may not be as reliable as it once was. So one day I decided that this book project had been taking me too long. I must write about my experiences. I made up my mind on a beautiful October day: I am going away for the weekend to write.

I gathered about ten library books about the civil rights movement and Dr. Martin Luther King and a few books about writing books. I packed up the books and my notes that I had been writing for months and drove to Red Top Mountain State Park, about forty miles north of Atlanta. Before leaving home, I'd called for a reservation and was told that no rooms were left. Reservation or not, I was so ready to write and to get to Red Top Mountain, which is one of my favorite places to get away, that I got in the car anyway. After a quick drive north on I-75, I arrived midday.

Before getting out of the car, I said a little prayer: "Oh God, I know that your Word says that we have not because we ask not. I am asking for one room for tonight so that I may work on my book." A request so simple, but God hears the simplest prayers. As I walked toward the desk, I could tell that the receptionist was having a hard day. Apparently someone needed four cottages. She was trying to make amends for the cottages that she did not have. She offered the person on the phone four lodge rooms instead. As I listened, I realized that if that person didn't want a lodge room, I certainly did. Well, the person on the phone was referred to the manager.

When the receptionist asked if she could help me, I said, "You could give me one of those lodge rooms that you were tying to give to the person on the telephone." Immediately she said, "I can give you one, but it's downstairs." I thanked her and accepted the offer. I preferred an upstairs room, but I was so happy to get any room at all that I went to my room with much gratitude.

As I placed my key in the lock, I sensed someone walking on the leaves behind me. I turned and, to my surprise, six deer were grazing in the leaves. I rushed inside, opened the drapes, and pulled a chair up to the window. For about twenty minutes, I watched the beautiful animals, only twenty feet away from my window. They inspired me so much that I began writing.

While at Red Top Mountain, I went over to the restaurant for a quick meal. A waitress named Jan inquired about all the books that I carried around with me. She asked if I were in school. I told her that I was writing my own book. She asked what it was about. I told her about my civil rights days of marching and protesting in the 1960s. This Southern white woman replied, "Oh, you are giving me chill bumps just talking about it. Please give me your card or your e-mail address so that I can know where to buy it. Our children need to know what you are writing about." Oh, how I agreed.

One of my motivations for writing this book is that my son Byron, his children, and the children of the future will have an idea of what my generation and others before me experienced. It's important for future generations to learn about our struggles as African-Americans. It is imperative for young people to know that "our freedom was not free."

If we don't teach our children, we will have to rely on Hollywood to make movies in which producers will give their version of history. I believe it is my lot to tell my part of the story, my version. One might say that no one else can reveal what I saw and felt, what I did, except me. Perhaps if I had written this book years ago, I could have recalled more memories. But I am much more mature now, of course, and I've had more recent experiences to pair with my past.

Someone told me to write only about my involvement in the Albany Movement. But I believe that I must tell the entire story of my life. A more detailed story can give readers not only a much closer, deeper look at my life, but I hope this will also personalize the history of the civil rights movement. This chronicle of my life can help others, especially young people, to understand the broad context and significance of the movement and how those of us at the back of the line moved up to the front to take responsibility and make contributions to the greater community. So, let's begin at the beginning . . .

Family History

My father, William H. Ward, Sr., was one of twelve sisters and brothers. His parents scolded him when he married my mother, Mary Lue Thompson, a beautiful lady who never finished elementary school because she had to work in the fields of various farms.

It seemed funny to me, but I was told that my father was supposed to get a "beating" because he married my mother without informing his parents and because they wanted him to finish school first. (He'd had a couple years of college at the time.) When his parents threatened a beating, my dad jumped up at the opening of the well. He promised that if his parents wouldn't beat him, he would come down and not jump into the well. I thought that it was a cute story about my parents.

My paternal grandfather, Charlie H. Ward, Sr. was the love of my life. Like my dad, my granddaddy was very reserved and somewhat quiet. I loved them both so very much. My paternal grandparents owned a farm with acres of land, chickens, hogs, and cattle. I went to visit them and spend the night quite often. I followed my granddaddy around the farm and watched him care for the animals and slaughter hogs to get bacon, pork chops, ham, and yes, "fillet of trotter" (pigs feet) and chitterlings (today's expensive delicacies). My favorite pastime was to get the eggs after the hens had laid them. My grandmother was an excellent cook. I thought that her best food was her chocolate marble pound cake. Often, I had watched her churn the milk and make butter.

Those were "the good old days," the days spent at my grandparents' house. Now my mom and dad are deceased. My grandparents on both parents' sides are deceased. Nevertheless, I must help my son, Byron, to realize what a blessing it is to know from whence you came. He, his children, and his grandchildren can read this book, long after I am gone.

I never knew my mother's mother because she died when my mother was a baby. It haunts me that I never saw her or even a picture of her. However, I remember my mother's dad, the Rev. William Thompson. He was a Baptist preacher who had a lot of fire in his delivery of any sermon. My ancestors were great role models. Now I have only two uncles left, my mother's brother Dempsey and my dad's brother, Thomas. It was my Uncle Thomas who allowed me to live with him during two summers of my youth. There are no aunts left on my mother's side. My only maternal aunt, Aunt Precious, is deceased. I still have six paternal aunts: my Aunt Doris whom I look like more and more everyday, my Aunts Vera, Jeannette, Helene, Shirley, and Mary whom I lived with as a teen. One paternal aunt is now deceased. All of my aunts were role models for me. However, my deceased Aunt Ella was the one who encouraged me to travel and see the world. I never forgot her advice. She believed, as I have come to believe, that the best textbook in life is to see the world with and through your own eyes.

One might ask, "Is it necessary to list all of your aunts and uncles in a book?" Well, the answer is yes because they have helped me along the way. There are hundreds of cousins, but some stand out in particular, like my maternal cousin Mary Roberts in the South and Karen Davenport from the North, whom I would visit in the summer and stay up talking to about our dreams and aspirations until the crack of dawn.

Childhood Memories

My earliest memories are rooted in Albany, Dougherty County, Georgia. Summers were so very hot in southwest Georgia. We would put on our tee shirts and shorts and wait for Mama to shower us, or as we would say "spray us," from the water hose. I remember the fun times—the games we played, roller-skating in the middle of the paved streets, turning cartwheels on the lawn, climbing trees, and playing house. The latter was never my choice. For some reason, I did not like playing house. When you played house you had to play the mama or the daddy. I didn't like to play the mother because the mother had to clean the house, wash the dishes, and take care of the children.

But I enjoyed playing school. I loved being the teacher. I spanked the imaginary students in my class when they became disobedient or when they answered the questions incorrectly. Playing the piano was another favorite pastime. I pretended to have a piano. I sat for hours playing imaginary keys on the windowsill as I sang. I really wanted to take piano lessons. So much so, I tagged along to piano class with my neighbor and best friend, Willie Faye Brown, whom I called Faye.

I always enjoyed dancing, too. My introduction to dance took place when I was in the sixth grade. Five of my classmates and I were in a tap dance routine. We had to purchase uniforms, including shoes. When I told my mother that we'd been asked to go to Buster Brown for tap dance shoes, she told me in no uncertain terms, "Child, you better use what you've got 'cause money don't grow on trees. I bought you black patent leather shoes for Easter. Now you go downtown and tell Mr. Daniels to put taps on those shoes." I was so embarrassed to think that my regular church shoes would be transformed into tap shoes. However, I followed my mother's favorite expression, "You need to make a way out of no way."

As a pre-adolescent, I was a tomboy. I loved to climb trees, especially one tree in our back yard. I would climb that big evergreen, find me a comfortable spot, and fall asleep in the tree. My mother would look for me on these occasions. When she could not find me, she would shout my name all around the house. If I didn't answer, her voice rang out across the back yard, "Gloria, Gloria, where is that girl now? If she is gone from this house, I'm going to kill her."

Now, back in the day when your parents threatened to kill you, that meant a severe whipping or beating with a belt, an extension cord, or a tree limb. If you think that the Department of Family and Children Services would be notified, think again. This discipline was considered appropriate in those days and in the community where we lived. This was medication to keep us "young ones" on the straight and narrow.

Even though I considered myself a tomboy, that did not stop me from playing with dolls. I loved it all, climbing trees, cutting out paper dolls, blowing bubbles, making mud pies, and as my mother would say, "the whole nine yards." I remember a time when my brother, Billy, and I tied a car tire to a tree limb. He helped me into the tire and began to spin it around and around. After turning and turning a few times, I became so drunk that "I was sick as a dog," as we would say in the South. I threw up for days. Never again! This was the "Six Flags" ride at our house, the black tire ride.

The very best times of my young life were sharing in the pillow fights with my sisters and brothers. The pillows did not hurt. Momma and Daddy could not hear anything except us children giggling and the sounds of us calling each other pet names. Pillow fights were quiet, there were never any bruises from being hit with a pillow, just a bruised ego. Along with a pillow fight, jumping in the bed was the best means of gymnastics and wrestling. We had a great time as children.

I shall always remember the good old days. There were so many of us. I have three brothers and three sisters. All of us were born at home except one. A midwife, Mrs. Mary Coley, brought us into the world. My parents lost one child, June Olivia, who died very young, probably from a fall with a head injury or from crib death. We never really knew. Mama always said she was too pretty to live. She was fair with red, curly hair.

My mother and father had their first six children very close together. This is probably why we were paired together quite often. Ernest and I were paired, then Barbara and Billy, then Carl and Ella Jeane. Unfortunately for my sister Cassandra, my parents had only seven living children. The odd number meant no sibling to pair off with Cassandra who was six years younger than the sixth, Jeane, as we called her. Perhaps this is why today Cassandra is so independent and a very private individual among all my siblings.

While living in my parents' house, we children had to sleep together. One slept at the head of the bed and the other slept at the foot. This was never a problem unless one of us wet the bed. When that happened, I was the one blamed. That is about all I will say about that.

My oldest sister and I slept together. Every night my sister attached a big safety pin to her pillow. Before we fell asleep, she pushed the safety pin in front of my face. "If you wet this bed tonight, I am going to stick you as though I am sticking a big balloon. You'd better not wet me, you hear? I dare you to cross over on my side of the bed," she would say as she drew a faint line with a pencil in the center of the bed to indicate what was off limits. It must have worked. Today I still have a tendency to sleep curled up in the pre-natal position on my side of the bed, a habit that started during childhood.

My mother and father belonged to a few society clubs in Albany. One day my mother was preparing a dinner that she would serve following a meeting. She was baking a chocolate cake when suddenly four of her children crawled out from under the table to claim the spoon. We all shouted, "The spoon is mine, the bowl is mine."

This was a high moment in the baking process when Mama would assign the batter-filled spoon to the youngest child to lick. Oh, what a treat it was to taste the cake before it was baked. The bowl also had some batter left in it for us to fight over. This may sound crazy, but we loved it. We had the best times of our lives. Eventually, we shared the batter. We stuck our little fingers in the bowl, scooped out all the remaining batter, and licked our fingers clean.

This act of sharing was our recreation. I think that sharing cake batter and sleeping together made us closer then and now. This is one reason why I could not have been a juror in the Michael Jackson case. Knowing what I know about children in a large family climbing in bed together would not help the prosecutor's case.

When there was a rainstorm with thunder and lightening, my mother gathered us all together in one bed. If not in one bed, we would all lie down on the floor, on what we called a pallet. We would hide under the covers, make a tent out of the covers, continue with pillow fights, complain about who pinched whom, and turn on a flashlight under the covers. But our fights made us stronger and closer, then and now. Today we are stronger and as close as we can be. Of course we don't continue our sleepovers now that we are grown, but sleepovers are not as bizarre to me because I come from a large family. Please read no more into that, other than what I stated.

A Blessed Childhood

My mother and father took very good care of my siblings and me. We had a very blessed life. We didn't have everything that we wanted, but we had far more than a lot of children. My mother, bless her soul, had a way of making everything work out for everybody. She knew how to make meals that would feed all of us. We never suffered from malnutrition. We wore neat, clean clothes. Sometimes my brothers would not have clean jeans to wear the next day. We didn't have a dryer, so my mother would put the boys' jeans and my physical education gym shorts and tee shirts on a split brown paper sack in the oven over night.

My mother could always find us lunch money in one of the many zippers in her pocketbook—not a purse, but her pocketbook, which was her safe deposit bag for emergency funds. I remember that my mother made many of her clothes and mine. My sister Barbara had clothes and shoes sent to her from our Aunt Ella, my dad's oldest sister, in New York. I was so sad that none of those clothes or shoes would fit me. I was happy for my sister, but I did envy her for all of the nice things that were sent to her from the fashion capitol at that time. The styles arrived at the big New York department stores months to a year before getting down to Albany.

I could not wear Barbara's clothes, but she did help me with my homework. She and my mother taught me how to speak and behave like a lady. Barbara taught me about personal hygiene and table manners. Barbara was the first-born grandchild and the first in our family to be a role model as a college student. She inspired me to go to college, typed my research papers, and furnished me with lunch money on most days. She worked at Albany State College (University now) in the dean's office and later as a librarian.

Barbara and her husband Hugh allowed us, her siblings, to come to their house almost daily and wait to be picked up after school by our parents. One might say that Barbara was a surrogate parent. To this day, her home is still the Grand Central Station for me and for all of my siblings and their children. What a responsibility it must have been, and continues to be, as the oldest of seven children.

After I graduated from Albany State and was working, Barbara decided to go to graduate school in Atlanta. She and Hugh leased their home in Albany to me. I shared this house with a roommate, Carolyn Williams (now Carolyn McCloud), one of my best friends who now lives in Dallas, Texas. Carolyn was the serious one, and I was the humorous one. I was a teacher, she was a speech therapist, and we shared a lot of good times together. Two other friends, Carolyn Reid (now Carolyn Brown) and Wanda McDuffy (now Wanda Vinson) also lived in our neighborhood then. I have so many beautiful friends, but these friends have been my friends for over thirty years. Even today in Atlanta, my friends are also my prayer partners. I cannot call the names of them all, so I will say that each one is special. I do appreciate their loyalty and their friendship. They are friends in the ministry and some are lay. Some are male, and some are female. Some are local, some are national, and some are international. I am not bragging about how many friends I have, but how many prayer warriors God has given me. Therefore, I say, "To God be the Glory.

Memories of My Father

My father was very sociable—the life of the party—when in the company of others. At home with us, he was easy going and quiet. But when we went to Grandma's house and to other places, he would talk. He was popular and he dressed very handsomely. A man we called "Salesman Sam" came by our house at least once a year to take measurements for my father's suits. He would also order shoes for my Dad.

My father had a couple years of college, but many spring and summer months he worked in Detroit, Michigan, as a brick mason because the pay there was so much better than in the South. And there were seven of us—many mouths to feed. We missed him so much when he was away.

He and his brothers learned the trade from their father. One of my father's brothers, Henry Ward, taught brick masonry at the Monroe Vocational Technical School in Albany for many years before his death. And my father taught brick masonry to my brothers.

My father and his brother, Charles, Jr., built very beautiful homes for their families. Unfortunately, with so many children to feed and seasonal income, the most painful thing in the world happened. My father lost the beautiful brick home that he had built in foreclosure. I hurt for him. (That is why I have so much compassion for many people who have incredible high interest rates on their homes, cars, and other purchases.) I was so concerned about my father. I know how hurt he was after building our house from the ground to finish.

A special bond existed between my father and me, perhaps because most people talked about how much I looked just like him, curly hair and all. His friends would say, "Ward, looks like you spit that one out." This was a popular expression when a child looks like the father. I always wanted to please my father and make him proud of me. I can't remember ever getting a spanking from my father, except one time. I don't remember what it was for or when. All I know is that if my daddy raised his voice at me, I would cry—I guess because I wanted to be the model daddy's little girl.

I shall always remember that he took me to my first baseball game. I must have been in kindergarten or first grade. I thought how cool the ballpark was with the high beam lights and the beautiful manicured grass. Who could have cut all that grass? We had a great time together, as the songwriter said, "Peanuts, popcorn and cracker jacks, I don't care if I ever get back." I was told that Albany once owned the team that was playing, a team called the Red Cardinals.

Another significant memory of my father involved a splinter in my thumb. My father took a needle and put fire to it, cleaned it with alcohol, and started digging in my thumb with the needle to get the splinter out. I cried and cried because the thumb was swollen and seemed to have started getting infected. I remember him saying, "Be still, Gloria, and trust me!" That was all I needed to hear, the "trust me" part. In an instant, the splinter was out. He gained my trust all the more.

I also remember how important my father was to me was when I was graduating from high school. I was one of the commencement speakers. As I stood up to begin to speak, I looked and looked for my father in the audience. Where could he be? Before I finished, I saw him coming in and I almost forgot my conclusion. I was sad that he was late but happy that he made it at all.

One of the hardest things that I have ever had to do in my life was to sit by my father's bedside in the Hutzel Hospital in Detroit and watch him suffer and cross over unto death in 1974. I was alone with him hundreds of miles from Atlanta. It fell my lot to buy a shirt and tie for him in preparation for his burial. Because of his drastic weight loss from multiple myeloma (a cancer of the bone marrow), he could not wear one of his own shirts. My father died only a few weeks before his fifty-fifth birthday, but he had become so frail and so small. I had to buy a shirt with a neck size of thirteen and a half, as oppose to his usual neck size of a fifteen and a half.

It was very difficult and painful for me to shop alone in Detroit and to make arrangements for my father's funeral. I took his suit to be cleaned, and I took care of every other detail. Thank God for a friend of his who supported me, Rena, and her son, Willie Morgan. Finally I had to prepare to have his body sent home to Albany. That was just as bad as the shopping. I was okay until reality stared me right in the face. I had to have my father's body shipped via cargo on a Delta Airline flight. After taking care of the business of shipping his body home, I had to catch my own flight back home.

The second hardest thing I've ever had to do was agree to place our mother in a nursing home for her own safety. She wasn't terribly ill, but she had difficulty swallowing and had problems falling. It was so difficult keeping her there because she desired to go to her house so much. She had always been very independent, so for her to depend on others was most difficult. Eventually, my siblings and I were faced with a conference with the medical staff. The doctor told us, "Your mother needs to have a feeding tube to survive."

What a difficult decision to make. After some dialogue, we voted six to one for the feeding tube. We decided that there was no other option than the feeding tube, or she would expire from the lack of nutrients and medications for her diabetes and other medical challenges. However, I often ask myself the question, "Was our brother Carl right to vote no?"

Our mother was eighty-four when she died in 2004. Another difficult thing that fell my lot to do in life was to speak at her funeral representing the family. My son, Byron, said, "Mom, I can't believe that you could do that—speak at your mother's funeral." In disbelief, he kept saying, "Wow, that's your mom! Man!" I would imagine that Byron felt that, since I have spoken at so many funerals that's one thing, but my mother's funeral was a different story.

On the other hand, one of the happiest of family times was a reunion of my siblings and our mother at Cassandra's apartment prior to my mother's decline in health.

Listening to Elders

As a child I often sat at the feet of the elderly. I enjoyed hearing them tell stories about their pasts, how they walked three miles to school in the rain, sleet, and snow. The best stories were about going out on dates, how they met their husbands or wives, or how long they dated. There were many stories about "making ends meet." It didn't matter the subject or which stories they told, I thought they were all so intriguing, to say the least.

I remember Mrs. Annie who lived behind us for many years. She was a very neat and organized widow who lived alone. For years I really thought that Mrs. Annie was related to us, but as it turned out we weren't related at all. She was a gentle, sweet, and loving lady who shared with us all of the time and most of my childhood days.

My mother and father had very elegant socials in our home and served dinner, usually a traditional meal of potato salad garnished with sliced boiled eggs and paprika, buttered English peas, candied yams, fried chicken, hot buttered rolls, iced tea, and chocolate cake. Just before a social was to take place, my mother always sent me to Mrs. Annie's house to pick up a package. I would run home with a grocery bag full of items that rattled and clinked all the way. I felt like "Mr. Tin Man." Before the guests arrived, my mother adorned the table with great silver and china. Then as I observed the beautiful table, I realized that we were not wealthy, as I had thought. We had borrowed the beautiful silver from Mrs. Annie.

Mrs. Annie often bailed us out when we were short an egg or a cup of sugar. She often helped us with lunch money. Mrs. Annie was an angel. Oh, how I loved her. I can't recall how or when Mrs. Annie died, but I do remember the pain of her death. And I'll always remember sitting on the porch talking to Mrs. Annie. I could not imagine my life without her. Everybody should have a Mrs. Annie as a guardian angel.

Then there was Mrs. Pattie, a very frail woman who lived about three streets behind us. She was my babysitter during the day while my mother worked. Mrs. Pattie cared for my brother Ernest and me. I guess that is one reason why he and I are so close. I'm only about eighteen months older than Ernest. Whenever Ernest dropped his bottle, I would suck on his bottle until I was caught.

Mrs. Pattie had a pot belly wood stove on which she cooked our breakfast. I can still smell her pancakes cooking and the aroma of burning wood and coals, and I can still taste her grits and eggs with a hint of butter. She fed my brother and me together. He got a spoonful of grits and eggs, and I would get my "helping." Eggs and grits together was the perfect breakfast. The perfect dessert was slightly cool applesauce with cinnamon.

It is amazing how older persons influenced my life. Ms. Elizabeth, my babysitter in the evenings when my parents went out for social events, also had a big impact on me.

Ms. Elizabeth was so pretty and young, probably between twenty-one and twenty-five at the time. I was so excited when she took me to the store and for walks because many people thought she was my mother. She had a beautiful brown complexion (We would say pecan tan.) and my mother was very fair complexioned. I too was pecan tan, though my favorite Uncle Bill had nicknamed me "Chocolate."

Evidently Ms. Elizabeth was a seamstress because one day she made me a skirt from the remnants of her own dress project. It was the prettiest gift that I can ever remember. Maybe I thought it was pretty because it was made especially for me, or maybe it was pretty because Ms. Elizabeth was pretty. Either way she made me so happy with my skirt of many colors.

One awful day Ms. Elizabeth told me that she was going to be moving away from Albany. She was going to Detroit. I didn't know where Detroit was, but it seemed a very long way. Just before she left, she took me shopping, and we wore outfits made of the same multi-color material. Many people complimented us on our outfits: "What a beautiful girl you are, and you have on a beautiful skirt just like your mother." Reluctantly, I would say, "She is not my mother, she is my babysitter."

When Ms. Elizabeth left, I was so heart broken. I knew I would never see her again. I often had thoughts of Ms. Elizabeth throughout my adult life. I wondered where she was and how she was doing.

Approximately five years ago I asked her sister, who had remained in Albany, for Ms. Elizabeth's phone number. It had been almost fifty years since I had talked to her or seen her. When I called, we had the best reunion on the telephone. She was around my mother's age, about seventy-nine years old. I told her, "Now that I have found you, I am coming to see you." She was so happy that I was coming to Detroit to see her.

Within two weeks, I checked into a hotel in downtown Detroit. I called her and made arrangements to see her. She took a taxi downtown to join me for lunch. We talked about her daughter and grandchildren. We talked about my family and career. Our reunion was such a warm, moving experience after all the years that had elapsed. To this day, Ms. Elizabeth, whom I now affectionately call "Momma Elizabeth," and I talk on the telephone every other month and send each other greeting cards for various occasions.

For reasons unknown to me, I have always sat at the feet of older people. People in my neighborhood would sit and talk to me for hours. My childhood closeness with older people undoubtedly is the foundation for the many beautiful friendships that I have had with seniors throughout my life. Since I moved to Atlanta, I have made new friends that have lasted for years. Some of the friendships have come as a result of church work and organizations. For fear that I will get in trouble for omitting the names of some, I will not call all their names, but they know who they are.

Nevertheless, I must pay a special tribute to one with whom I shared a very special bond, Mama Julie, for almost thirty years in church and at family gatherings. My friendship with Mama Julie is the one that I remember the most. I found myself with Mama Julie and her family for most holidays and for her birthdays. During the good times and the bad times, we were on the telephone and in each other's presence. She called me her "other daughter." Mama Julie's children were and remain my friends. Although I love her family, two of her children, Dot and Ike and I have shared a special bond for about twenty-six years in church and at family functions.

I cherish my relationships with senior citizens. The conversations that I have them afford me the opportunity to absorb more wisdom. I am like a thirsty sponge in their midst. Some others who have impacted my life and ministry are Mrs. Lelia, Sister Daisy, Mother Elizabeth, Mrs. Thelma, Mrs. Elizabeth, Mrs. Eunice, Bro. Henry, and Deacon John, who have special places in my heart, just to name a few.

I believe that my friends who are senior citizens have helped me to become the leader that I am today. They encouraged me in my projects and in my ministry. I cannot name all of the senior citizens who have encouraged me as I moved from the back of the line to the front of the line over the years. However, I thank God that He has placed them in my life for such a time as this.

Although I dedicate this book to the younger generation of this country, I owe a special debt of gratitude to the senior citizens who have impacted my life. And, yes, I owe a debt of gratitude to those whom I do not know. Additionally, there are those who have impacted my life and do not desire to be called senior citizen. Nevertheless, I thank God for their inspiration in my life and for the wisdom they imparted to me.

3

Headquarters at My Mt. Zion

"Be confident of this very thing, that he which hath begun a good work in you will perform it until the day of Jesus Christ." . . . Philippians 1:6

Mt. Zion Baptist Church was my church from birth. From my earliest days, my parents carried me to this church where they were members. It seemed as though it was the biggest place I had ever seen, other than school. As I grew up, I realized that church can make you or break you. I was determined that I was somebody. I was the Sunday school secretary. I read the minutes many Sundays. I was a part of the Baptist Training Union (BTU). Later on I learned that it is not your position in church, but your walk with God.

Everybody who was successful seemed to attend my church. Some would say that our Mt. Zion was a "bourgeoisie" church. Our pastor was the Rev. Dr. E. James Grant who served until I became an adult. Many of my teachers attended Mt. Zion, including my seventh grade teacher, Mrs. Mary Frances Jenkins, my dentist, Dr. Ed Hamilton, our attorney, C.B. King, and the editor of our newspaper, *The Southwest Georgian*, Mr. A.C. Searles. Yes, Mt. Zion was and still is the church attended by many of the elite—some may say the "the movers and the shakers." My mother attended and my immediate family still attend the new Mt. Zion where "all walks of life" are ministered to Sunday after Sunday.

As children, sitting with Mom and Dad, we had to behave, be still, and not be "fidgety." Mom sometimes gave us her favorite Beechnut gum in the yellow wrapper to keep us quiet. Or maybe it was to keep our breath fresh. Either way, it kept us awake. During the 1960s, there were five of us siblings, which meant that Mom would tear one stick of gum into five pieces.

Elementary school children sat with their parents. Children weren't supposed to look around or toward the back. That was impolite and could cause you to get your legs slapped or your ears twisted. I could not wait to become a teenager so I could sit in the back of the church or in the balcony. In fact, I would ask to go to get water from the water fountain so that I could see who was in the back—any excuse to get up and look around.

As the youth of the church, we sometimes sat in the last pew until one day we realized that the women in white or blue uniforms were suppose to sit there. They were the ones who passed the shiny gold and silver plates from pew to pew to collect the offering. They wore nurses' white shoes and nurses' white hats and treated us as though we were in a library. They walked with one hand behind their backs and told us "Shhhhhhhh" all of the time. "Quiet! Rev. Grant is getting ready to preach." They were doing their jobs.

We had many programs at Mt. Zion, including the Birthday Club. One day I signed my name for March, my birth month. I thought surely I would be getting a birthday gift in March. Only later did I discover that we had to pay lots of money to compete with the other eleven months in raising money for the building fund.

I enjoyed church, but there was so much to learn, such as when to sit and when to stand, how to sit still, how to be silent, how to listen to the choir, how to listen to the pastor, and for goodness sake, remember not to point. There were many do's and don'ts: Do not kick the back of the pew. Do put your offering in the plate. Don't forget to put the change in the silver plate and the dollars in the gold plate.

When everyone stood up to sing, this was the congregational hymn. It seems like only yesterday, but all the voices singing sounded so pretty and so powerful. Sometimes I saw people in the choir and in front of me crying as they sang. I don't recall when I stopped sitting with my parents and my siblings. But I do remember one Sunday when I was twelve years old. When we sang a powerful hymn entitled "Love Lifted Me," something happened to me. I felt as if I would fly away.

Rev. Grant was singing along with the choir, and he began calling people to come and surrender their lives to Christ. I had heard about Jesus, the Christ, in Sunday school and in BTU. By the time I sang the third verse, I found myself walking down the aisle of the church. I heard people clapping and shouting. My pastor told me that he was proud of me. He asked me lots of questions. I can't remember them all, but I remember one very well. He asked me if I wanted to be baptized. I told Rev. Grant, "Yes, sir."

I don't know where my mother or my father was on that Sunday. Perhaps my mother was on maternity leave and my father was working in Detroit quite often. However, I remember Rev. Grant saying, "Tell your mother we are going to baptize you on the fifth Sunday. Tell her to get you a white dress, a white towel, and some white socks. I am going to baptize you. Do you hear?"

"Yes, sir," I replied.

After church, I told my mother what Rev. Grant had said. I was so disappointed because she didn't think that I understood what I had done. My mother phoned Rev. Grant and asked him to wait. She didn't think that I was ready. I wasn't baptized that fifth Sunday. Some weeks passed, and I took that same long walk down the aisle to answer God's call through Rev. Grant.

This was the moment. God had sent me back to get the baptism that He desired for me. Soon thereafter, I was baptized, clad in white. I repeated the words that Rev.

Grant asked me to say. I confessed to Christ and repented of my sins, which now I know comes out of the Word of God. The words of Paul in Romans 10: 9 read, "That if thou shall confess with thou mouth the Lord Jesus, and shalt believe in thine heart that God hath raised him from the dead, thou shall be saved."

I struggled with Rev. Grant because I didn't want him to hold my nose as I went under the water; I wanted to be in control of my nose. Because of that lack of trust, I learned a lesson. I believe God allowed just enough water to get into my nostrils to teach me a lesson or two: Follow your commanding officer. Nevertheless, there are times that I am too trusting of people today.

My baptism at Mt. Zion was a milestone in my life. This was my church, and since I had confessed Christ, this was my salvation. This was the beginning of my new life in Christ Jesus. This meant that the beautiful red leather Bible that my mother had purchased from a traveling salesman for me was to be read by me, and the Word of God had to be applied by me. As I read the Word on the pages and noticed the pretty pictures, a whole new world opened up for me.

That red leather Bible has special meaning to me even today. People who grew up outside the South may not realize how common it was for traveling salesmen to appear at our doorsteps with expensive Bibles. The red leather Bible was a big deal and a big investment at that time. My mother questioned me about whether or not I would actually read it if she purchased it. But I really wanted that Bible, and she did buy it for me. I feel that she planted an early seed into my current ministry. Who knows? Had she not purchased that Bible, I may not have become a minister.

After my conversion experience at age twelve, my life was strangely different. I found myself more tolerant. I didn't like to criticize people. I wanted to help people, and I didn't want others to hurt or to criticize others. I had strong convictions about injustices and about the mistreatment of people in general. My mission in life seemed always to work for and speak out for the underdog.

High School Church Girl

My parents expected me to study and make good grades. Most parents wanted the same for their children. As a high school student, I did study and earned good, not excellent, but good grades. (Good grades come from scanning your homework or giving it a cursory glance. Study means spending time with homework for an hour or two.)

During my sophomore year at Monroe High School, I was so happy that I was among the first students to enter the new school. I was in seventh heaven. The whole school was new—new chairs, new equipment, new library, new cafeteria. I had a new attitude. All ninth graders were to remain in junior high, which is now called middle school. I was no longer a ninth grader. I was in *high school!*

I was somewhat popular. I had friends in my own grade, but most of my friends were in the senior class. This was because my best friend and neighbor Faye, who lived behind me, was a senior. When Faye went to the movies, she asked my parents if I could go. When her family had reunions and family gatherings, I attended. We were the best of friends. We studied together. I used her encyclopedias. Faye had many sisters and brothers, as I did. They were like my big sisters and brothers away from home. I could talk to Faye about anything. As a matter of fact, she handed down her training bra to me. Now that is a good friend.

Many of Faye's friends became my friends. One night she had a backyard dance and her senior friends were there. Everybody danced and had a great time. I was a wallflower because no one would dance with me. That's what happens when you try to grow up too fast. No one seemed to notice me. I reminded myself that I was still skinny and ugly, although I thought God had brought me through those feelings. I had a tremendous crush on Larry. He treated me like the child that I was. He danced with me just to be polite and I knew this. Everybody treated me like a child. I did not like that! I wanted to be one of them, to be accepted. I was always "little sis." (I now believe that students should hang with youth in their age group. This keeps one from growing up too fast and from feeling inferior to the older girls.)

I was not only younger, but I was also a girl who went to church. Very few boys wanted to hang around "church girls." I guess church girls would speak in an unknown tongue to them—the language of the Holy Bible.

I was so sad when Faye and the others graduated. I felt so alone and dejected. Now I had to find new friends in my junior year. The highlight of that year was the junior-senior prom, which was to be held in the gym. Youth today would not entertain the idea of their prom being held in a gym for a New York minute. When we were in high school, however, facilities were segregated. There were no downtown ballrooms open to "colored" children for the proms, as students have today. If there were one saving grace, I guess it was that we saved an enormous amount of money by having our prom in the gym.

My Introduction to the Movement

During my days at Monroe High School, Mr. Melvin Heard was principal and Mr. James A. Hopson was the assistant principal. Our homeroom teacher, Miss McCree L. Harris, was my French teacher as well. In Miss Harris's homeroom we learned a lot about the civil rights struggle that was going on throughout the country. Miss Harris told us about Dr. King and about the injustices that were done to people of color. She kept us informed about what was going on in Greensboro with the sit-ins and in Alabama with the marches and protests. For a while, those places seemed far away.

But before we could blink an eye, the smell of freedom was in the air in Albany. We knew of Albany State College students who courageously took it upon themselves to organize and march to downtown Albany, cross the Flint River Bridge, and protest the segregated Trailways Bus Terminal. Arrests were made and many of the students' educations were suspended. Yet they were very serious about stopping segregation and putting a choke hold on the injustices in Albany.

Adult leaders began to put their heads together. Organizational meetings were planned by some of Albany's movers and shakers, including Dr. William G. Anderson, Atty. C. B. King, Mr. Marion Paige, Mrs. Goldie Jackson, and others. Out of their strategy meetings, the Southern Christian Leadership Conference (SCLC), Student Nonviolent Coordinating Committee (SNCC), and other groups, the Albany Movement was born. Rallies took place with mass meetings at Mt. Zion Baptist Church, led by Dr. E. James Grant, Pastor, and Shiloh Baptist Church, led by the Rev. H.C. Boyd, Pastor. (Old Mt. Zion Church, founded in 1865, is now the Civil Rights Museum. The new Mt. Zion Baptist Church is flourishing under the capable leadership of the Rev. Dr. Daniel Simmons.)

These churches were considered the headquarters where singing, praying, and planning took place. Mt. Zion was the church where I grew up and was baptized, so I really felt comfortable there during the mass meetings. As an influential teacher, Miss Harris and her family were instrumental in my getting involved in the Albany Movement. At these rallies, I heard the facts as they were presented. But segregation had already had its effect on me personally from my experiences growing up in Albany.

Dr. Martin Luther King, Jr., was described as a "drum major for justice." Since I was a cheerleader in high school, I took it upon myself to become a "cheerleader for justice." This was a very important position to have, I felt, because it afforded me the opportunity to join in the mass demonstrations, to march, to kneel, and to pray for the walls of segregation to come down. This position afforded me the opportunity to sing, to clap my hands, and to prepare for the mass meetings to start. Most days after school, a group of students met at the church prior to the meetings to get the people in the mood for marching or for whatever we had to do. When I left school those afternoons, I had a made-up mind that I would be there to make a difference for my people.

4

Cheerleader for Justice

"Let your speech be always with grace, seasoned with salt, that ye may know how ye ought to answer every man." . . . Colossians 4:6 (KJV)

In the South of my youth, things were separate but they weren't equal. Blacks could not enter the front doors of theaters, restaurants, bowling alleys, etc. Everything was segregated, including my doctor's office. Water fountains had signs that read "Whites Only" or "Colored Only." The water fountain for whites had refrigerated water. Water from the "Colored Only" fountain had the worst tasting water you could ever drink or imagine. Rest rooms were separate and clearly labeled with signs that read, "White Ladies" and "Colored Women."

I shall never forget going to the doctor's office. I walked into a waiting room furnished with a beautiful sofa and chairs, exquisite tables and lamps. I heard the relaxing piped-in music. I saw new magazines all lined up on a table. As I stopped to select one to read, I was told to continue on to the back room. It was a hole in the wall with three ladderback chairs, a couple of torn books, a mop, a broom, and a bucket. I'd been told to sit in the janitor's closet. Black folk had to pay for services rendered, too, so what is this?

The zoo was segregated. The parks were segregated. When I took my little nephew Joel to the Chehaw Park Zoo, he saw the Chehaw Amusement Park and asked me to take him "over there" so that he could ride on one of the go cars.

"We can't go over there," I told him. He cried, "Why not?"

The more I tried to explain why he couldn't ride there, the louder he screamed. How does one explain that other children can ride at the amusement park, but he cannot because of the color of his skin? This was the straw that broke the camel's back for me. On that day I became infuriated about the segregated system that had a dual standard in serving the public at public facilities paid for with public funds.

Restaurants were also segregated. I recall one in particular, the Artic Bear, the equivalent of an upscale McDonald Restaurant today. A big animated bear outside of the restaurant rotated slowly as he licked his ice cream cone. Every boy and girl's dream was to go to the Artic Bear. You could order hot dogs, hamburgers, pies, milk shakes, and ice cream cones. (Of course, the Jimmy Hotdog was the best in town—ten for a dollar. The Jimmy Hot Dog Stand was on the south side of Albany in Harlem.)

On Saturday mornings, my mother would take us to the laundromat right behind the Artic Bear. She had a way of getting us to help by promising us a treat at the Artic Bear. Well, we would go, but unlike the white folks, we had to go to a window in the back for services. Whites would get their order from the front window.

This irritated me so much. Of course, getting an ice cream from the back window wasn't too bad. If we complained too much, we'd hear, "Go home without ice cream." My siblings and I learned to adjust readily. What did not settle with me was why the white folks had milk shakes and we had ice cream cones. I learned later that it had everything to do with economics. My family could only afford ice cream cones with seven children in the picture. We learned to thank God for the little bit. It was no wonder that when I had my own child, Byron, we went to all the fast food restaurants and ordered whatever we wanted. This was the least I could do for him, and it was a blessing for me to relive my childhood in a better society.

Ready for Change

After a childhood of climbing trees, licking cake batter, and pillow fights with my brothers and sisters, I was ready to make a serious difference. By the time I was a teenager, I could hardly keep my mind on my studies. As the songwriter says, "I woke up this morning with my mind set on freedom." I had an overwhelming desire to make a difference in the lives of my people. I wanted to have some input in bringing about change that would have to come to the controlling powers, the leadership in my hometown of Albany, Georgia.

I knew about the initiative that brave students at Albany State College had taken. They had come forth very strongly determined to make changes in our very segregated town. The college students had rallied, marched, chanted, and stormed the segregated bus station. The Interstate Commerce Commission (ICC) had ruled that there was to be no segregation on the buses. Blacks could sit anywhere on the buses. Sitting in the back of the bus was no longer the order of the day.

I had witnessed on television and read in the newspapers about Rosa Parks, a beautiful, courageous seamstress in Montgomery, Alabama, who had refused to give up her seat on the bus to a white man. In spite of ICC rulings, there was still opposition by most whites. Many blacks tested the new ruling and were harassed and given looks of disapproval. The looks and the unkind remarks from whites were not major problems. The major problems came, however, when vindictive evil spirits lashed out with acts violence of brick throwing, and, yes, bombings. Bombings took place all over the South in retaliation to court decisions to desegregate the buses, trains, and all public transportation in this country.

As high school students we could not sit back idle and do nothing. With the college students, we knew we could make significant changes. "Freedom riders" came to our town from all over the country to assist in our crusade for justice. With the freedom riders and "Freedom Singers," we were determined to make a difference in this county, especially in Albany. Many people were key players in this effort, but there also were others who would not get involved.

When the Albany Movement called for a boycott of the stores, especially during Christmas time, we agreed to "buy black" and not patronize predominantly white stores like Woolworth's Five and Dime, Belk's Department Store, Rosenberg's, and others. For the Christmas season and for Easter, most of us wore black armbands and black clothing rather than new clothes. At first, the impact of the boycott was not very effective because some blacks would sneak into those stores or cross the picket lines and ride the buses anyway. But as this became more obvious, more people began to join the picket lines and the boycotts.

The paradoxical thing about segregation was that white people wanted nothing to do with a black face or black hands, but they loved and respected our green dollars. As a matter of fact, there came a time when the merchants wanted Police Chief Pritchett to intervene because the merchants' sales had fallen off so much that the businessmen were running scared. I have seen letters that were written by white merchants pleading for help from the Albany police.

As black people, I now believe we came to realize how much power there is in the almighty dollar. Our dollars, our voices, and our withdrawn service in the workplace made quite a statement. We wanted those in power to know that we, too, have power. I thought of the words of the Apostle Paul who said, "I can do all things through Christ that strengthened me."

When I participated in the Albany Movement with my friends and classmates, however, I had no idea that what we were doing was making a positive difference and making history. But we were very serious about what we were all about when we talked about the upcoming mass meetings during our forty-five minutes lunch periods at school.

I remember our first mass meeting. There was singing and praying as we prepared for the leaders to come into the pulpit. We shouted, "Freedom, Freedom, Freedom, we want freedom now!" The mass meetings reminded me of how coaches get team members fired up. The chants, the rocking from side to side as we sang, kept our adrenalin going. When the leaders came in, we were very excited about what would be said. The church was usually packed to capacity crowds, with many standing in the balcony.

We heard the stomping of the feet, the rhythm and singing of the crowd, with the voices of the Freedom Singers above the crowd. That was a sound that made you want to do something, do anything to end this horrible thing called legal segregation. The crowd sang in unison. When the electrifying voice of Rutha Mae Harris and the Freedom Singers rose above the crowd, however, there was the unusual feeling of being inspired, of being motivated, of being energetic. Mae was never shy about "bringing the house down," as we called it. In fact, she loved to sing and continues to this day to sing freedom songs all over the world.

The Pain of Discrimination

Over the years, I've thought a lot about my personal experiences with discrimination. Everybody seems to have experienced some form of discrimination in life. People discriminate against you because of the color of your skin, your background, your ethnicity, your gender, or your religion. Discrimination is a dirty disease. Its symptoms last a lifetime. More than that, it is painful and it lessens your self-esteem.

When I was in high school, I participated in the chorus, in the band as a majorette, as a cheerleader, in student government, and in the drama club. My favorite activity of all was my participation in the drama club. My instructor was Mrs. Julia Craig Mitchell. She was a fantastic instructor. When I became a teacher, I tried to imitate her style of teaching. She was articulate, poised, personable, and sharp.

In my sophomore year, Mrs. Mitchell produced a major play. I was working behind the scenes, but I wanted a speaking part so badly. Mrs. Mitchell promised me that I would have a speaking part in a year or two. She tried to use her seniors first. My junior year was a little bit better because I had a part with narration in the Christmas Pageant. I wanted to be an actress in this pageant so badly, but there was no part for me. As fate would have it, the Virgin Mary became ill with the flu, and Mrs. Mitchell had to replace her. I asked to play the role, but was told that the Virgin Mary had to be fair complexioned. I was crushed. After searching for a replacement, Mrs. Mitchell said that she would allow me to play the part, but I would have to keep my scarf on my head and drape my face with the scarf as much as possible. This was not intended to discriminate, but that was how some blacks viewed things then. Some felt that the Virgin Mary must have been white or fair like the pictures displayed in books.

The pain of discrimination did not always come from white people but from blacks as well as my favorite teacher. I still love her to this day. Mrs. Mitchell never knew that I was offended. I never voiced my feelings about it. But many children from all over the world and throughout the years have been emotionally hurt by references to their skin color and the length or texture of their hair.

When we were in high school, some of my classmates had a saying, "If you are white, you're all right; if you are brown, stick around; but if you are black, get back." Back in the day, women of a darker hue had a difficult time. Not only did whites discriminate against you because of color, but some of the sisters and brothers discriminated against African-Americans who had darker skin color. With curly hair, you were more acceptable. Well, I had one out of two, with my curly hair. I know that some of you who read this book will say that this is not the truth. Trust me, every bit of this is true.

Television was also responsible for fostering some of our prejudices and discrimination. During my days in school, television programs mostly showed beautiful women who were white with flowing long hair. I had neither. I was and am still "chocolate colored brown." My uncle Bill, one of my mother's brothers, called me "Chocolate." My brothers and sisters were different hues. I was one of the "brown ones." TV commercials showed white and fair-skinned people. They were the ones to represent beauty. Somehow I believed some of it. I had low self-esteem for a long time.

As I grew older, I began using make-up. But most of it was much too light for me because it was manufactured for women of a lighter hue. When I put on make-up, I looked as though I belonged in a mistral show. When I purchased silk stockings, I could never find them dark enough for my legs. My mother taught me how to change of color of the hosiery. Most people may not know this, but if you want darker silk hosiery or pantyhose, you can change the color by boiling a couple of tea bags in water. After the color is deep brown, you drop your stockings or pantyhose in the tea. This makes a perfect shade for women of color—"tea bag brown."

Today there are all shades of brown make-up and pantyhose to match the complexion of all women. Praise God for those manufacturing companies who keep women of color in mind for their products. Thanks for the companies that hire women of color to model the products.

Majorettes and Other Forms of Discrimination

Another form of discrimination took place when I wanted to become a majorette. The same kind of discrimination affected homecoming queens and the like. Girls with fair skin and long hair were sought after as the school queens. Back in the day, it seemed that black and brown women were not considered. Today, however, we are a little bit better. Our image has changed. There are so many beautiful women of color. I am proud to be a woman of color. As a child of the King, I know who I am, and I know whose I am.

Speaking of queens, during my high school homecoming, I was able to win the title of Miss Senior. But there was some mix-up about the real winner. One sponsor said that her girl won. My sponsor said that I had won. I felt awful about this. How could the both of us wear the title of Miss Senior. Who would ride in the front of the convertible car at the homecoming parade? My sponsor, Miss McCree Harris told me firmly, "Ward, you are Miss Senior. Get in the car."

Mrs. Barbara Darden said that her girl won and told her to sit up front. Well, that left the backseat for me. At least that is what I thought, until Miss Harris told me to get out of the car. I followed her instructions because it was time for the cars to get in the procession. She told me, "Ward, get up on the hood of the car. You are Miss Senior, and you will ride as the queen today."

I did indeed look just like the queen sitting on the hood of the car. To my surprise, I had no idea that the car's engine would make the hood so hot. The temperature on that hood must have soared to 125 degrees. I was cooked, shifting from side to side and alternating my hands for the queenly wave expected of a homecoming queen. During my lifetime, I have had some serious drama. I was a drama queen.

Finally, there is one type of discrimination that I have simply ignored. I attended a bible school for a couple of years in Atlanta. Although I was a pastor at the time, I was not permitted to take classes in pulpit ministry because the school did not sanction women pastors. Women were not allowed to take courses related to preaching at Carver Bible College. I took the classes prescribed, but one day I simply quit because of that rule. I then attended the Interdenominational Theological Seminary (ITC). However, in the midst of a semester, God through His Spirit had me to return to the bible school and I stayed to graduate. I didn't really want to, but I obeyed God. Since that plan of obedience, I have completed the Masters and the Doctoral degrees in Pastoral Studies at Covington Theological Seminary with God's help. All the times that I faced discrimination, I could hear the Holy Spirit say to me, "Stay focused. Don't give up and don't give in."

As a matter of fact, I had similar concerns about writing this book. I have always had to pray and encourage myself in the Lord. I tell myself: don't worry about what people say to you or what people do to you. It's all about recognizing who you are in Jesus. Stay focused, "don't give up and don't give in." Remember the words of Paul in Philippians 4:13, "I can do all things through Christ which strengthens me."

Deep Roots of Self-Esteem

With all of us, I think, self-esteem takes root during childhood. Many of my childhood memories shed light on my own self-esteem growing up as a black girl in the South. As a child, I saw myself as ugly. I thought that I was the Godzilla of Albany, Georgia. The models on television, the models in newspapers and magazines, all played a part in my poor self-esteem. My understanding of inner beauty came much later.

At age fifteen I was tall, so skinny, and in my opinion, so ugly. I had such a low self-image. Maybe my negative feelings stemmed from having brothers and sisters who teased and criticized me. We all criticized one another. It was like a game in which we competed to see who could give the most ridiculous descriptions. My siblings and I had a habit of calling each other names and describing each other's appearances. We talked about each other's noses, hair, feet, lips, eyes, etc.

This was fun, teasing one another, until one struck a nerve or hit below the belt and described the truth about someone. The truth always seemed to hurt. I had had very spacious teeth. One sibling had hair that was more coarse than the rest of us. The list goes on and on. Nevertheless, we all grew up to be pretty decent-looking brothers and sisters.

My older sister Barbara and my older brother Billy attended Hazard Elementary School on the campus of Albany State College; it was attended by children of many of the elite families and college professors. My other siblings and I attended Hansel and Gretel Kindergarten, which was on the other side of town. I believe that the "grassroots kids" attended Hansel and Gretel. Nevertheless, I loved my school. I loved my teacher and director, Mrs. Ruth Hall.

I was very hard on myself as a child because my mother often compared me to my beautiful older sister, Barbara, who was very popular and in college. My mother bragged on Barbara often and said, "Why don't you be like Barbara, walk like Barbara, do this or that just like Barbara?"

Barbara could sing, and she practiced singing opera and classical songs all the time. She was a majorette and very shapely. I guess I could not wait for my body to grow up so that I could look like her. Barbara was short and I was tall. Barbara was light-complexioned and I was dark. Her feet were small and my feet were big. These comparisons made me think that I was ugly, not to mention that I had spacious teeth. My sisters and brothers teased me that I had a "lie gap." This made me so self-conscious that I found myself never wanting to lie about anything or seldom wanting to smile.

I never seemed to get past "my ugly side." Of course, television didn't help my negative self-image with the "all-white blondes with the flowing hair" images. Not to mention that I received the same type dolls for Christmas year after year—white Barbie dolls. Even my sweet mother, Mary, was very fair with Native American features of beautiful high cheekbones. Her complexion had an orange tint to it. I found out very recently that she had Cherokee blood running in her veins. I asked her on her deathbed if she were Cherokee, and she answered, "Yes."

From that day to this current time I have been researching my Native American heritage as well as more of my African-American heritage. As I sought my Native American connection, I have learned so much. Recently a very dear friend, Dr. Margie de la Rosa, Chief Little Star Moving, of the Native American Tsalagi House in Mount Vernon, New York, conferred upon me my name in Tsalagi from the Cherokee glossary.

She said, "Everywhere you walk, you deposit wisdom. You are always creating situations where people can learn from you. Therefore, I am conferring upon you the name AGATANAI ADASTI AGIYA. Your name means Wisdom Walks Woman." (Wisdom = Agatanai; Walks = Adasti; Woman = Agiya.) I will forever study to learn more, so that I can impart wisdom to my son, Byron.

Family Resemblances and Early Influences

Some people would compliment me about my "beautiful, smooth, brown complexion and my curly, wavy hair which would draw up after braiding it. My hair was identical to my father's hair, which was so wavy and pretty. He didn't put chemicals in his hair to make it that way, either. People in my church said that I was "a spitting image" of my father, William, whose skin was a "pecan brown tan" like mine. I believe that I was teased about my color's being different from my mother's. Who knows for sure? Was it color? Was it the teasing? Was it the childhood accident?

When I was eleven or twelve years old, I was accidentally burned when my beautiful sister, Barbara, spilled hot chicken grease on me. I sustained second-degree burns to my left shoulder and left arm. I especially missed my father during this trauma because he was away working in Detroit.

The long healing process did not help my negative feelings about myself. Burns can be terrible trauma, both physically and emotionally. They leave scars on your body and scars on your mind. Burn victims hurt so bad and for such a long time. Nobody wants to admit it, but burned skin smells horrific. Nobody wants to be around you. Insects follow you, and you feel so undesirable, so unloved, just awful.

One Christmas, I remember, we did not get many presents. I watched my mother "shuck corn." Shucking corn is strictly southern, as far as I am concerned. It is the act of pulling the corn silk off of the cob. I would put the silk together and tie a piece of paper around it to hold it together. Then I'd stuff the corn silk down into a Coca Cola bottle to make a doll. Is it any wonder that blonde, man-made dolls made me feel a little inferior?

When my father purchased our first television from one of our white neighbors, this was the beginning of watching more and more blondes on television. No, this did not help my self-esteem. I thought that in order to be pretty, I had to be a blonde. Not until years later did I realize, through psychologist Dr. Kenneth Clark, that African-American girls had been programmed to love blonde, white dolls over black dolls.

Speaking of that early television, I remember that we placed three colors of cellophane on the screen to make it a color television. The blue cellophane was placed over the top, representing the blue sky, the red cellophane was placed in the middle, and the green was placed at the bottom to represent the green grass. As we see today, someone carried this idea all the way to create a major invention, the color television.

We now have black dolls, as well as dolls of all other ethnic groups. We have come along way. There are "Bobbie Dolls" for girls and some for boys, too, if they choose to collect dolls.

At school, things were a little bit better than the teasing I got from my siblings. At school, your peers begin to tell you that you look good. Deep down inside, however, you have to search yourself and weigh things. You begin to notice what is beautiful to you. Then one day, it hit me that beauty really is more than "skin deep." Beauty is more than a skin color, more than a pointed nose, more than blonde hair, or more than blue eyes.

With time, my self-image improved. After hearing others say that you are attractive time after time, and after being voted a class queen and being selected as a majorette and a cheerleader, you find yourself not being so hard on yourself. And when you begin to see your features in your mother, in your father, and in your sisters and your brothers, you begin to feel that maybe you don't look so bad after all. More importantly, when you can feel the love of God inside of you, others can feel that same love coming from you. Love can make you feel beautiful and cancel out all the ugly that you feel.

Beauty is within. You are as beautiful as you think that you are. It is your spirit that makes you beautiful. I have seen beautiful women in my lifetime and their spirits are so negative that that beauty leaves them and leaves you with a sour taste in your mouth. God is the Creator of mankind. We have been made to carry the genes of our parents, and we are to be grateful for we are God's creation. "We are fearfully and wonderfully made."

Regarding this whole issue of self-esteem, I want to explain my feelings about beauty a little further. One of my favorite television shows is "Extreme Makeovers," a program where individuals are chosen to have their bodies altered to enhance their looks. Some individuals come on the show with a desire to change their facial features, their noses, their teeth; some come to have a "tummy tuck." The changes go from one extreme to another. This is good if you can afford it, but what about individuals who cannot afford an "extreme makeover?"

I say we can get our teeth cleaned, exercise to walk off inches and pounds, and eat the proper diet for our health. These are the minimums that do work. Even a change of hairstyle, a change of eyeglasses, and, yes, a change of one's wardrobe. However, let me make this one confession: I was so tired of my spacious teeth. I wanted what some would call an extreme dental makeover. My dentist told me that he could help me. After a few visits, the permanent work was installed. When this was done, I was so relieved that this was completed. Next it was time to look in the mirror.

When I looked into the mirror, I almost died. This was not what I had envisioned. My dentist, who was a friend, asked me how I liked the work. I could not speak. I don't like to hurt people if at all possible. Finally, I said that I didn't believe my husband would like this new look. This was how I left it because the work was permanent, and there was nothing that I could do.

On my way home I cried and cried. I knew that my husband, Dan, would not like the new look for two reasons. First of all, he has always liked the space between my teeth. He'd told me, "Natalie Cole has a space between her teeth. She is beautiful and so are you." The second reason was that the teeth were thick and bulky, somewhat opaque and not thin enough, as my natural teeth were.

So there you have it, Gloria with the new look. I did not like it and now that I don't like it, you really won't be able to make me smile. I do believe my husband hated to look at me, and I could feel his dislike for the dental work that I was "stuck with" for awhile. What must I do to please my husband? Best advice: Buy the best when investing in cosmetics.

My husband has a thing about individuals taking care of their teeth and gums, and about oral hygiene in general. The discussion about my teeth became such a bone of contention that I had to seek further help or risk being divorced. Well, maybe divorce would be a bit extreme. But, believe me, this was a big deal in our house. Ask him, and he will probably disagree and say, "Not really."

After a few years passed, I made up my mind to seek another professional, a dentist who could find a way to make my teeth beautiful. I was not concerned about me being beautiful, but about finding a way to make my teeth beautiful. My plan was to take a beautiful spirit of God on the inside and couple it with beautiful teeth. I sought a dentist who specialized in orthodontics and prosthesis. I was determined to replace the dental work that my husband and I did not like.

I told the new dentist what I had done and what I wanted done. I signed a contract to do the work over. He was so positive, and we bonded quite well. It was interesting that he, too, was from south Georgia. The dentist took impressions of my teeth and sent the requested work off to a lab. When the work came back, he wasn't pleased and sent it back. I was very impressed with his work. The final result was all worth it. My husband was happy and so was I.

We still make trips to the dentist often for cleanings and x-rays, and we send our son Byron as well. My husband made sure that Byron's teeth were taken care of and improved by wearing braces to correct his teeth. During the two years of wearing braces, my husband took Byron for his appointments faithfully. The office was about twenty-three miles away. I took him only a few times because his daddy made sure he would take him. I relate all of this to say that we have to take care of our bodies, our minds, our teeth, but more importantly, we must take care of our souls. We must feed our hungry souls the truth and the Word.

We must give our attention to our Creator. It is God who has made us. However, since my friends belong to the three Abrahamic faiths, Judaism, Christianity, and Islam, I can say that we should find ourselves in our churches, mosques, and synagogues on the respective Sabbath Days. We must take care of our physical, mental, and spiritual bodies.

(L-R) Dr. Wright's mother Mrs. Mary Lue Ward, a woman of wisdom and a homemaker. Mother crossed over in 2004 and Mr. William H. Ward, Sr., her father, was one of the best masonry contractors in the South. Her father crossed over in 1974.

(L-R) William H. Ward, Jr., Gloria Ward, and Barbara Ward (siblings) pose for the camera one Easter morning before church. Gloria was approximately four years old.

As high school student, Gloria Ward poses for a photograph in her cap and gown at seventeen. Counted one in the top 10% of her senior class, she was one of the speakers for graduation in 1963.

The Ward sisters and brothers stand together the day of their mother's funeral in October 2004. They are standing from the oldest to the youngest. From left to right: Barbara W. Carroll, William H. Ward, Jr., Gloria Ward Wright, Ernest J. Ward, Carl F. Ward, Ella Jeane Ward, and Cassandra D. Ward.

Mr. Daniel W. Wright, Jr. shares a special and happy moment with his wife, the Rev. Dr. Gloria Ward Wright, on her 7th Pastor's Appreciation Sunday.

Byron Ward Wright's graduation day at the University of West Georgia. (L-R) Mom, Byron, and Dad.

5

Life Lessons

"For he shall give his angels charge over thee, to keep thee in all thy ways." . . .
Psalm 91: 11 (KJV)

When I saw many of my friends driving cars, it looked so simple. Then I watched my older sister Barbara learn to drive. She backed the car out of the driveway and—bam—she took down a whole brick pillar. So I was a little apprehensive about learning to drive. I was not going to ask my parents for driving lessons. I was too smart for that. Their answer might have been a resounding "no!"

At the time I had a crush on Yoyo, a cute "dark chocolate" teenager who had returned to Albany from New York. He had an old car with gears. I really don't remember what model or make, but I do remember that he made an exceptionally good driving instructor. Yoyo came to town just as I had broken up with Rabbit, the love of my young life. I had dated Rabbit much too early in my high school days, from ninth to eleventh grade. As fate would have it, Rabbit, who gave me the nickname "Tater," started dating an older student. Suddenly I was wondering if I would ever date anyone else again. Since that painful experience at such a tender age, I really don't advise long relationships in high school, especially for ninth and tenth graders.

Rabbit was excellent in football, basketball, and track. His participation in sports seemed to have been his greatest priority, more than participation in classroom activities. Rabbit and I had attended the school dances and marched in the mass demonstrations together. I was very close to his family and his sisters. One of his older sisters, Miss McCree Harris, was my homeroom teacher and homecoming sponsor. She was a big influence on me. She made me aware of the discrimination and the injustices in our city, introduced me to the Albany Movement, and encouraged me to attend the mass meetings. Although Rabbit and I had dissolved our relationship, we remained friends and products of the Albany Movement.

College Bound

My senior year of high school was interesting and challenging. My grades had fallen somewhat, but I was a good student and was passing in my classes because I was intelligent and articulate. But I needed higher grades for college. (As I've often told my students since then, if you allow yourself to fall short in any semester of school, that will impact your grade point average and other things.)

In my junior year, 1961-1962, I went to jail four times, but the real challenge for me came during my senior year. This was the most crucial year of high school. City-wide tests were required; if you were sleepy or not present for the preparation of such tests, your scores were affected and you really suffered in the long run. Many of my classmates failed their course work, and some did not graduate on time or graduate at all.

My parents had always pushed for us to go to college so there were to be no more marches, just classes and studying to improve my grades. I started thinking really hard when my classmates said that they had been accepted at prestigious colleges and universities. Many would boast about scholarships offers from Yale, Harvard, Brown, New York University, Spelman, Morehouse, Fisk, and the list went on . . . Then it hit me like a ton of bricks. My plan was to attend college, but I had not yet applied to any university or college.

I considered myself blessed and highly favored. I made up my mind that I wanted to go to college. It was time to make applications for college and for scholarships. I had a very good average, but not impressive enough to generate a scholarship.

When my sister Barbara had attended Albany State College (now Albany State University), she had applied for a loan of some kind. All I ever heard was that she was waiting for her student loan to go through. Later I found out that she was in a work/study program.

I continued to do some very heavy-duty studying. I wanted to graduate, but it seemed that so many obstacles were interrupting my goals. I had some friends who walked to class with me on the second floor of our school. (Be careful who your friends are because sometimes you will be led to places you had not intended to go.) On the way to class one day, teachers were standing in the hallway awaiting the arrival of the students. My friends and I saw a new male teacher standing in his doorway. He was one of the youngest faculty members. I said to one of my friends, "Wow! he's so cute."

One of the girls said, "I am going to tell him what you said." And she did tell him. From that day on, I passed by his class smiling. A few times I stopped and talked about the current events or the weather. Needless to say I had a crush on this man who was single and handsome.

On occasions "Mr. Frank," I will call him, gave me a ride home, and before long we began to date. Can you believe a student and a teacher? At this time I was seventeen-years-old and he was twenty-two. It was not a good idea, but he decided after meeting my parents that he had better talk to his principal before someone else did.

Mr. Frank went to see the principal, Mr. Heard, who was having lunch in his office. As Mr. Frank began to explain that he had fallen in love with a student and was going to propose to her, he mentioned my name. Mr. Frank told me that as soon as he said, "the Ward girl, Gloria," Mr. Heard's fried chicken wings commenced to fly into the air. Mr. Heard knew my family well.

Mr. Frank told me that the principal seemed pretty cool with the idea, however, because my parents were made aware of the relationship. Mr. Frank gave me a beautiful solitaire diamond engagement ring for my birthday that March. His proposal was the talk of the high school and of the town. Some teachers thought that this would probably end his career. That did not happen. However, the pressure became so great that one night after a basketball game, he found all four of his tires were flattened. I think that some of my friends took part in that act of vandalism. I believe that pressure came from the school board eventually and that Mr. Frank was brought behind closed doors, as we say down South, and was called on the carpet. He did not resign but made himself scarce, and I saw less and less of him.

When graduation approached, I was in the top ten percent of my class and selected as one of the commencement speakers. I felt that God was giving me a chance to have honor and dignity. The marching, the protests, the arrests, and the times in and out of jail, had begun to take effect. I saw changes that had resulted from the Albany Movement. The movie theaters, restaurants, and other public facilities were integrated, and voter registration was encouraged.

I believed that I had made the best contributions to society that I could make. I had made my commitments to the Albany Movement. Now it was time for some personal commitments—time for Gloria to catch up for time had been fleeting. I had slept on the concrete floors of the jails, taken that infamous ride in the paddy wagon, and tried my best to make it through school and make it through this engagement that seemed so right at first.

It did not seem like it, but I had lost so much time being distracted and being out of school during the demonstrations. Don't get me wrong—it was worth it. I had not lost interest in school, but I did not feel as secure about going to school. What was going to happen to me? When graduation took place, I was just so happy that it was all over.

I decided that I needed a break so I went to New York to spend the summer with my maternal aunt, Ella, the traveler and artist. Her specialty was oil paintings. She was the one who wanted me to travel and see the world. She did not want me to get married. She and my Aunts Doris, Shirley, and Mary encouraged me to go to college. After working in New York at a co-op, packaging twelve-inch-long beef tongues in cellophane wrap, I was convinced—Go to school, Gloria! Wrapping beef tongues was not my idea of a career. This was a wake-up call for me.

I returned home and got in the National Student Defense Loan line to try to qualify for a loan. I did get a loan, which would pay my tuition. Upon graduation, I would not have to pay it back if I taught school. Each year that I taught would cancel out much of the loan.

At Albany State, I did well as a freshman. I continued to live at home, made good grades, and made new friends. God has a way of working things out in God's timing.

One day as I was driving my Dad's car home from class, I saw Mr. Frank driving a very attractive young lady who turned out to be a former Miss Albany State College, Miss Annette, who had been very active in the Albany Movement as well. I called Mr. Frank and inquired over the telephone about what I had witnessed. At first he said that she was a friend. I knew better. Eventually, he told me the truth. I had taken the ring off a few weeks prior to that. It was for the best. All things work together for good, for those who love the Lord according to His purpose.

I studied hard, made friends with energetic and intelligent students. I became popular after being at Albany State College, and I went on with my life. I learned many lessons along the way. Thank goodness, I knew the Lord and had a prayer life throughout my school days. The Bible says: "The prayers of the righteous availeth much."

In 1966, I was voted "Miss Junior" at Albany State University, apparently because some thought of me as attractive, humorous, and somewhat intelligent. I pledged Delta Sigma Theta because my sister, Barbara, my Aunt Shirley, and my Aunt Mary were all Delta sorority sisters. But I later changed my mind about pledging so that I could focus on my studies. While majoring in sociology with a minor in psychology, I was able to secure a six-week internship with Family and Children Services in Atlanta where I worked with unwed mothers.

I had thought that I might one day that I might end up as a social worker after training in that area. Nevertheless, good common sense and the Holy Spirit advised me to take some education courses. With those courses, I knew I could teach, which was a secret love that I had. And, of course, I knew that for every year that I taught, I could cancel out my debt to the National Defense Student Loan. I was to graduate in 1968, but I took some additional education courses that delayed my graduation to 1969.

Out of College and Into the "Real" World

After graduation from college, I planned to leave Albany and relocate in New York. One day I found myself at home, ironing my clothes and packing a footlocker in preparation for leaving "the good ole city," when a very dear friend came by to see me. Alton Moultrie and I grew up together throughout high school. We had a crush on each other that we allowed to stay dormant. Alton respected me and I him. He was and remains like a big brother to me.

Alton came by that day to tell me that our alma mater, Monroe High School, had an opening for a sociology instructor for the seniors. He knew that I was sociology major in college and had taken some education courses. Alton assured me that if I gave Mr. James A. Hopson my resume, I would get the job. But I wanted to move to New York. He asked me to apply and, if I didn't get the job, I'd move to New York. I agreed and within a week I had a job teaching sociology at Monroe High School. I called Alton and thanked him for his advice. Now that I had a job, I felt the need to move out of my parents' house. After a few pay checks, I bought a new 1967 blue Fiat. Then I found an apartment where many college professors lived.

I was a young twenty-one year-old high school teacher, working with some of my former instructors. (By this time Mr. Frank had moved on. I was told that he had entered higher education and the corporate world.) I was truly blessed to have that kind of opportunity. As a teacher, I performed well and received good evaluations. The students related to me, and I really enjoyed teaching, even more than I'd enjoyed playing teacher in my childhood.

Today many students do not appreciate their teachers, but the teachers who were considered the meanest and the hardest of all teachers were the ones whom I believe God choose to place in my life to make sure that I succeeded. Many great teachers and principals made sure that I walked the "straight and narrow," as my mother used to say. To this day, I continue to have contact with a few of my teachers. Mrs. Mary Frances Jenkins, my homeroom teacher and English teacher in the seventh grade, inspired me to be the best that I could be as a student. Today, as an author, she has inspired and motivated me to complete this book. Mr. James A. Hopson was my civics teacher and my second high school principal. He succeeded Mr. Melvin A. Heard. Yes, Mr. Hopson was the one who interviewed me for a teaching position and helped me to succeed in life. Mr. Hopson was a very spiritual, honest, and decent man who taught interesting social studies lessons. He was one of the male teachers who was very respected by me and taught me moral values. He was a great male role model for my classmates and me. Mr. Charles P. Mobley, my college instructor, taught world history and gave me my first thoughts about seeing the world and historical sites. He was an encourager and, more importantly, he had faith in me that I would one day succeed in life. Who would have thought that I, too, would teach world history?

Travel and Love Life

Throughout my lifetime, I have attracted some beautiful, intelligent, and strong men. Some confessed that they loved me. As a young adult, I dated some very interesting and brilliant black men. Relationships were good, and some were not so good. Nevertheless, I am not one for throwing away people. Therefore, I have continued in friendship with some of them.

Unfortunately one such friend, whom I fell in love with, was a friend of my father. As a child, I had admired him for many years. He was years younger than my father, but he was married. After coming to the realization that my feelings and his feelings were inappropriate, I chose to leave Albany and move to Atlanta to start afresh. Even though this happened when I was young and foolish, I did manage enough nerve to ask his wife to forgive me. More importantly, I asked God to forgive me. You see, this is very hard to write. The raw truth hurts deeply. If I had not left Albany, if I had continued to do wrong, God would not have blessed me as He has done.

I had some savings from teaching in Albany when I decided to move to Atlanta. But to save some money, I checked into the Paschal's Motel until I could find a job. After being there a week, I ran into one of my best high school friends in the lobby. Juanita J. James and I had gone to jail together during the Albany Movement. She asked me where I lived and was shocked when I said, "Here, in this motel." She invited me to live with her, and we shared her apartment for about two months until I found a job.

In Atlanta, I began attending Shaw Temple and joined an actors' guild where Samuel L. Jackson was a member. I performed in two major productions under director Andrea Frye. My last role was that of Angela Davis. We performed for three nights at the downtown Alliance Theater. I thought that I wanted to be an actress and live a very different life, but changed my mind when I fell in love with Jesus.

After moving to Atlanta, I made some bad relationship choices, but my prayer life helped me to walk the straight and narrow. I know that God forgave me for every sin that I have committed. His Word tells me that if I will confess my sins, He is willing to forgive me. He has done that. God has blessed me to remain in love and married for twenty-five years to Daniel W. Wright, Jr. Most of my friends know that this has to be a miracle from God because our marriage has survived the seven-year itch. God also blessed us and gave us a son, Byron, the best thing that ever happened to me. My family life with Dan and Byron began with my love of travel.

My destiny has afforded me many opportunities for travel and higher learning. The best classroom, I believe, is the world. There is no book that can take the place of traveling, one of my favorite pastimes. I love to visit new cities, observe new cultures, eat exotic food, and see what God has done in another corner of the world. Perhaps the beautiful hotels are attractive because of my years living in a segregated society.

The most extensive trip that I have ever taken was when a friend and I went on a thirty-day excursion via Eastern Airlines, an airline no longer in existence. My friend Jewel and I visited several places in the thirty-day period. I had studied places that I wanted to visit, and we put our two itineraries together. We traveled to New York, Puerto Rico, Dallas, Acapulco, St. Thomas, St. Maarten, St. Croix, and Hollywood, California. We had a great time until we ended up at a nudist beach inhabited by free-spirited, French-speaking people. Their spirits were too free for me. I ran like a cheetah from the beach back to the hotel.

When I met Jewel, I was new to Atlanta and did not know many people. She introduced me to a lot of teachers and principals, many beautiful men and women who worked hard in our community. Because we were both educators, we planned our trip around a teachers' conference, the National Education Association Convention, held in Dallas that year.

Jewel was a delegate to the convention, and I went as a non-delegate observer. I wanted to learn more about this teachers' organization. Interesting topics regarding classroom teachers, students, principals, and administrators were discussed at the convention. I was pleased to be a member of this prestigious organization. During long meetings at the Representative Assembly, I sat in the visitors' observation section and listened intently to the issues that were being discussed. This was a new beginning for me—a long way from Albany, Georgia.

I had not known Jewel very long, but she was friendly, humorous, and knew a lot of people. We met at a campaign party. She made me feel like a debutante coming into society for the first time. She was like a big sister and became a dear friend. Jewel was a few years older than I, but she was young at heart. She introduced me to several NEA members and some of her colleagues. Nevertheless, she was careful to keep the wolves away, guys with the wrong motives.

I was somewhat naïve—originally from a small town. Some of the young male teachers would ask Jewel who I was. She would tell them, "Go away, fresh man. She's not interested in you." Jewel was very protective of me. I didn't mind that. Sometimes at conventions, men and women too find themselves in compromising positions. Although I was single, I was not interested in the male educators whom I met. I had just come out of a relationship. For me, the convention was part of a thirty-day educational experience.

After we had been at the convention a couple of days, we were walking from the convention center to visit some receptions for candidates running for office. On our way, I became very hungry. I just wanted to go to someplace quiet, sit down, and have a meal. Most of the candidates' reception refreshments were only cheese and wine. I was not a drinker, but I did love to eat.

I was growing very impatient, which is unusual for me, but I was so hungry. As we continued to walk, an extremely distinguished looking man walked slowly toward us. He was wearing a blue jump suit and seemed preoccupied, but Jewel introduced us anyway. Our eyes began to speak a language that I could not comprehend. Just as I began to tell myself that I am here for a learning experience, I felt a little light and airy. As we continued to walk, someone offered us a ride. We headed to the nearest restaurant where we all made light conversations and snacked.

Later that night, I asked Jewel, "Who did you say that guy in the jump suit was?"

"Oh, his name is Dan, and he is happily married."

"Oh, really?"

"Yes, oh really!" she replied.

A ball was held on the last night of the convention, and it was a beautiful affair. I shared a table with Dan and some other people. Many delegates at the ball danced with each other. I danced with Dan many times, and he danced well. He was a perfect gentleman. Everything went fine, and we all enjoyed the ball and the convention.

As new friends, Daniel W. Wright, Jr., and I exchanged business cards the day that everyone was to return home. I had mixed emotions because I'd had a beautiful time at the convention. I was also experiencing jet lag and Montezuma's revenge.

Jewel and I were Atlanta-bound. I had really enjoyed myself, but I was troubled because I had character and integrity, and I had thoughts about Dan. I remembered what Jewel had said about his being happily married. Of course, Dan did treat me as though he were married. I was still on cloud nine because he was so good-looking, so nice and kind. I really asked God to forgive me for my feelings toward this man.

When I returned to Atlanta, I was hospitalized for about three days because I was dehydrated from the Montezuma's revenge. I did not give Dan a thought because I was preoccupied with feeling better. On the second morning in the hospital, I received a telephone call. He had found me. He inquired about me and offered his concerns about my hospitalization.

After I was released from the hospital, Dan began to call and tell me about himself. He asked me if I had a significant other in my life. I really did not at the time. He began to refute what Jewel had said about his being happily married. It turned out that Dan was an eligible bachelor and had not told the general population. I learned later that Dan is very private. More than likely, he will not like the invasion of his privacy for this book.

We began to date. We commuted between Atlanta and Savannah, where he lived and worked. This started payments to Ma Bell for many long distance telephone calls, as well as frequent miles on Delta Airlines. We also became innovative about meeting each other half way. The approximate halfway point between our homes was Macon, Georgia.

Dan continued in his position as a school counselor in Savannah. He also served as a board member on the board of the National Education Association (NEA). A native Savannahian, he is a life member of the National Association for the Advancement of Colored People (NAACP). Among many contributions made in the area of civil rights, he was president of the Chatham County Teacher's Association that integrated the Manger Hotel in Savannah. He was among members and friends of the NAACP at the January 24, 1964, dinner meeting that marked the first time African-Americans received open service as guests in any previously all-white public facilities in Savannah.

While we dated, I continued as a high school teacher in the Atlanta public school system and was a member of the (AAE) Board, the Atlanta Association of Educators. We dated for several years. We shared a lot and traveled to Toronto, Hawaii, and other places. We attended balls and banquets held by sororities, fraternities, and educators' associations.

Dan and I had so much fun together that it was frightening. I began to think, "What if we date for years and years? What would we do with our feelings for each other? Wow! Did that mean that I would marry yet again?"

At that time in my life, marriage was not a high priority for me mainly because I had been married twice before. The first time I married Raymond, a very handsome and loving Army veteran, when I was a twenty-two-year-old high school teacher. Raymond was very supportive of me. He had a sense of humor, and he loved cars and racing. My interests were a little different. Not to mention that I was afraid to settle down.

Raymond was from a big, close-knit family who believed in having children. I did love him, but I was scared to death of being married. The thought of getting pregnant and having babies was definitely a "No, No" for me. I wanted to be a star. During summers and on some weekends, I was a singer with a group called The Vivacious Velvelettes. Rutha Mae Harris, Jean Givens, Queen Esther Buckner, and I sang at the American Legion and various nightclubs in neighboring towns. On one occasion, we sang the background for a recording entitled "No Particular One" by Jessie Boone and the Astros.

I was determined that one day I would move to Atlanta and sing and become an actress. I felt that, since Raymond and his family were very strongly in the church, I was not the one to fit in. Instead of being interested in the church, I was interested in going the opposite way. I knew the Lord and I had given my life to Christ at age twelve. But the nightclubs and the good life seemed to be for me at that time. So after a very brief time I tried to have the marriage annulled, but I found out later that divorce was my only option. We were married only about seven months.

I divorced a perfectly good man who remains single to this day. George Raymond Proctor, a friend of my family, who was and is still committed to the Lord is serving as a deacon in his church. I thought that he and his family were too "holy" for me. He was committed to the church and loved the Lord, but later became committed to the Lord. I ran as fast as I could from the very one who loved the Lord. Ironically enough, I later became in love with the Lord and began to serve the Lord in the church as a witness for the Lord. Who would have thought that, after all of the running, I would run right into Jesus' arms?

My second marriage was a little different. I was introduced to a "church man," a socialite from Cleveland. A friend and church member called me one night to say that he had a friend in town, Dr. Fred, who was a "seasoned man" searching for a wife. My friend hounded me to go out with this man who was several years my senior. The next day, I did meet the gentleman. He was an educator with a doctoral degree in education. By now, I was tired of the night life, tired of meeting guys who were good, no good, and sometimes up to no good. Finally, I met someone who was settled, secure, and who didn't want children. Sounded like a plan to me.

We dated for a short while and then came the big diamond ring and the kind of proposal seen in movies or on television. Soon I was traveling back and forth to Cleveland. I resigned my teaching job to move to Cleveland. Shortly thereafter, we had a wedding that most women dream about. Dr. Fred and I sailed to the Bahamas for a honeymoon and moved into his penthouse overlooking Thistle Down Horse Racetracks in Warrenville Heights, Ohio.

Soon I fell into a deep depression. Something did not feel right. I sought professional help in this regard, which many people in similar situations don't do. I realized that I had made a hasty decision. Once again I was married, and this "feeling of flight" came over me for the second time in my life, only this time I wanted to make the marriage work. If only I could move back to Atlanta, I thought, some of my depression might be resolved.

Finally it was apparent that this marriage should not have taken place. This time, I approached things with a little more maturity and lots of prayer. I was very unhappy in my situation, especially now that I was miles away from family and friends. Then one day, out of the clear blue, Dr. Fred asked me if I were unhappy. I was ready and happy to tell the truth.

Now I was certain that there is a God. Only God would prompt that particular question. I told Dr. Fred that I was very unhappy and regretted giving up my job, my family, my friends, and giving up Atlanta. As I continued to stare at my unpacked boxes, it finally happened. Dr. Fred and I had a heart-to-heart talk. After our very candid discussion, we agreed that he would have my belongings shipped back to Atlanta. I asked my sister Jeane to help me to drive my car back to Atlanta.

Dr. Fred and I had the marriage dissolved after about six months. The marriage ended just as a business contract would end with terms, stipulations, and agreements. I left Cleveland without reservations or hesitation. When I returned to Atlanta, I secured another job and my own apartment. Fortunately, I even retrieved my old telephone number. I felt that my life finally had some normalcy in it.

I thank God today for the two beautiful African-American men who impacted my life. They respected me, and I gave them respect in return. I have much to bring to the table about relationships. After two failed marriages, I had and have nothing but respect and great admiration for these two men who were once briefly in my life. A very dear lifelong friend impacted my life for years. I did not marry him, but I would have married him in a heartbeat, for keeps, but God did not will it so.

I am not proud of all of the decisions that I have made throughout my lifetime. Of course, if I had to do it all over again, I cannot say that I would not repeat what took place in my past. I do know one thing, however. I know that God loves me and that God forgives me for every sin and every mistake that I have ever made. For me to admit my successes and failures to the whole world just might be a huge mistake. However, God has prompted me to do so. There is one thing that I know about the truth: The truth can set one free. I find the truth to be liberating. As President Franklin D. Roosevelt once said, "We have nothing to fear but fear itself." I can say that I have nothing to be ashamed of, but shame itself. Since I found Jesus, made Him Lord of my life, and accepted Him as my Lord and Savior, my Messiah, I have been liberated. Yes, I have been set free. Could you tell the whole world your life story? If you could, would you?

My prayer is that those who read this autobiography will be honest with themselves. Be honest about your passions, about your aspirations, about your idiosyncrasies, about your prejudices, and especially about what you desire for your life. When you do, life is so much sweeter.

Never Say Never

I went through years of never thinking about marrying anybody again. I had decided that maybe some people are never meant to marry. As soon as I had resolved that I would never remarry, I discovered why people often say, "Never say never."

As Dan and I dated for several years, we realized we had a lot in common. We traveled to many places together—to Toronto, to Hawaii, just to name a few, and we attended social functions together. Dan and I enjoyed each other's company. Dancing was one of our favorite activities.

After nearly four years of a "long-distant courtship, we finally decided to get married. We were married at 6:30 A.M. in my pastor's back yard on June 27, 1981. I felt that if Dan were serious he would be there bright and early. I was very interested in having a prayer breakfast, which we had in the basement of the home of my friend and pastor at the time, the Rev. Dr. George B. Thomas, who is now N'dugu T'fori-Atta.

Because Dan and I had been married before, we kept our wedding very simple. We invited only fifteen guests to our wedding and prayer breakfast. On our wedding day, I wore a powder blue dress, not a white dress as some divorcees inappropriately wear. My bridesmaid was Sarah, one of my very bright students who was like a daughter to me. We had a wedding reception a few weeks later at my church, Shaw Temple A.M.E. Zion Church. This was the same church where I did my trial sermon and served as the associate minister for many years.

When Dan and I were dating, the subject of children naturally came up. Dan had three children, two boys and one girl, from his previous marriage. When we decided to get married, I told him, "No children." I never really wanted children as some women do. Dan replied that every woman desires a baby—that is the purpose for a woman's life. And being Catholic at the time, he wanted children.

Well, Dan convinced me, but we had an age difference and I didn't have time to waste. I became pregnant at thirty-seven, seven months after we were married. I was told that most women in my age group should have amniocentesis, which can detect abnormalities. I refused to have the test because I knew immediately that I was carrying a healthy baby. In the seventh month, God spoke into my spirit that our baby was a boy.

Byron Ward Wright was born at Crawford Long Hospital around 6:30 p.m. He weighed seven pounds, one ounce, and was twenty-two inches long. When he was born, I cried, "Oh how precious. You look so familiar!" I had never seen anything more beautiful. I cannot describe how beautiful. I cannot describe how happy he has made me. We gave him my maiden name, Ward, as a middle name because I wanted to honor my father's name.

I thank my husband for helping me to walk in my destiny. God created woman to have children. I thank God and my husband for helping me to see the light. My son Byron is the greatest blessing to me. I don't know how I would be today if I had not had him. I am a better teacher, a better pastor, and a better person because I became his mother. After becoming a mother, I interacted with my students with more compassion, but more importantly, I saw God, the Creator, from a new and refreshing perspective.

Because of a very serious, unnecessary surgery earlier in my life, I had been told that I might never have a baby. Several of my friends urged me to sue the doctor. An attorney friend pleaded with me to sue the doctor. I told my friend that I would pray about it. After much prayer, I decided not to sue. I just believe that God gave us Byron because I did not sue. I could never prove this, but in my spirit I believe it.

Today our miracle child works in the music marketing business. Bryon completed a Business Administration Degree in Marketing from the University of West Georgia during the summer of 2005. Thanks be to God, we have a wonderful son. My belief is that Byron will one day have a legacy left by his parents that can make him proud. Perhaps, one day he will explain to his own children about their grandparents.

If I hadn't loved to travel, I might not have met Dan nor given birth to Byron. Over the years, I've enjoyed other benefits of travel as well. I have been to Canada: Vancouver, Montreal, Toronto, and Windsor. But my greatest traveling experience was to the Holy Land: Jerusalem, Tel Aviv, Dimona, Nazareth, Bethlehem, and the Dead Sea. I also spent an interesting time in Rome, Italy. The most comfortable travel was in London, I guess because there was no language barrier. I have traveled alone by train. I also traveled by train through the French countryside with a friend, Karla Bailey, who is like a daughter to me. She was an excellent guide and taught me many things about London and France, including lessons on the exchange of currency. Yes, I praise God for young friends and for older friends alike. I do love my friends. Proverbs 17:17 says that a friend loveth at all times.

6

Gloria and Kay:
Forgiveness and Friendship

"Let all bitterness, and wrath, and anger, and clamor, and evil speaking, be put away from you, with all malice: And be ye kind one to another, tenderhearted, forgiving one another, even as God for Christ's sake hath forgiven you." . . .

Ephesians 4:31, 32 (KJV)

One warm summer evening back in 1962, Mt. Zion Baptist Church was full to capacity for a civil rights meeting. Cameras and news commentators were everywhere because Dr. King had come to lead marches and prayer vigils. Press people had traveled to Albany from all over the country.

The youth and I were in our usual place at the front of the church where we were singing, clapping our hands, and chanting freedom slogans. Suddenly a distinguished looking white gentleman, with pen and notepad in hand, approached me. He introduced himself as Associated Press reporter Dan McKee and asked to interview me for a newspaper article. I was shocked. I did not have a clue about why he wanted to interview me with all the choices that he had. He said he was impressed with my enthusiasm as he observed me singing.

Mr. McKee escorted me to the vestibule of the church, asked me some questions, and wrote down my answers in his notebook. I told him about my arrest experiences and my beliefs about nonviolent demonstrations to end discrimination. I told him, "I will give up my life for freedom and the children I hope someday to have." At the time, I had no idea what would become of my remarks.

Within a few days, a huge article was published in newspapers across the country. Mr. McKee had interviewed two very different Albany teenagers: me—the civil rights demonstrator—and Kay Smith, a white eighteen-year-old who opposed integration.

Photos of us accompanied the story. My picture had been taken while I was singing at that mass meeting.

We lived in the same town, but Kay and I didn't know each other. I attended Monroe High School, "the Negro school." She had just graduated from the all-white Albany High School. (Her class turned out to be the last all-white class to graduate from that school.) Kay was the daughter of a conservative newspaperman and devoted to the ideas of the Deep South. She reflects now as an adult, "I was proud of that. I thought the world would be better off if schools were never integrated, if black people kept their place in society."

When out-of-town reporters descend on any town, they usually head to the local newspaper to make contacts. Mr. McKee met several local newsmen including Kay's father, an editor at the *Albany Herald*. When Mr. McKee proposed interviewing a white and a black teenager on opposite sides of integration, Kay's father suggested that Kay be the white teen.

Mr. McKee, Mr. Smith, and Kay met at a segregated downtown restaurant for the interview. Kay recalls, "I had the courage of my convictions and didn't hesitate to let the world know how I felt." In the article, she criticized black teenage demonstrators for being "fools" and "pawns" of the civil rights movement. She thought marches were "useless" and the jailing of demonstrators didn't "bother my conscience at all."

The interview appeared in the *Macon News* on Aug. 3, 1962, but never appeared in the *Albany Herald*. Copies of the article were sent to Kay from Macon, Norfolk, Va., and several other places. *Sepia* and *Jet* magazines also picked up the story. Kay received hate mail. She now recalls, "It troubled me that people would say such ugly things about me. But it never occurred to me that I was wrong . . . [The newspaper story] really portrayed me as what I was. That's the way my family felt. It was the way we lived our lives, and we really were convinced that white people were superior, and we had a way of life that would be turned upside down and on its ear."

The Years Pass . . .

After these articles were published, years passed and most people who read them probably forgot them. But I kept the articles for decades and used them as the focus of presentations during Black History Month. When I was invited to speak to my son's black history class at Warren T. Jackson Middle School, I showed students copies, as I had done at many other schools. On this particular day, I told the group that I would love to know what had happened to Kay Smith, the teenage racist quoted in the articles. It had been thirty-five years. What was she doing? Where was she? This took place during the month of February, 1997. To my great surprise, on the day before my birthday, March 8, 1997, I was at home, taking notes and studying for a test when the telephone rang.

The caller was my old high school friend, Alton Moultrie, the one who helped me to get my first teaching position. He was working in Atlanta with the Georgia Department of Industry, Trade, and Tourism. Alton had just met an *Atlanta Journal-Constitution* reporter who asked about me when she learned Alton had grown up in Albany, my hometown.

Alton told me that he'd just met someone I might remember but had never met. "Her name is Kay Smith. Now she's Kay Smith Pedrotti. You want to talk to her, Gloria?"

"Of course, I would! I've often wondered what became of Kay Smith, and I would love to talk with her. Give me her number." I called Kay immediately.

Our phone call was very emotional and filled with tears. We arranged to meet for the very first time a week later. We went to lunch and took pictures. People at surrounding tables began to stare at us, so we announced our story to the whole restaurant. Waitresses and others came over to our table. We showed them the 1962 newspaper article and talked about what had happened between 1962 and 1997.

The lunch had its light side, too. We both ordered chicken, a drumstick and a breast each. When the waitress brought our plates, she joked, "Sorry, we can't mix white and dark meat." We laughed, and Kay said, "You can if you are chicken."

At that lunch Kay asked me for forgiveness. I gave it but said it wasn't necessary. "You are in Christ and you are a new Kay. You've already been forgiven." She also told me what had happened to change her segregationist teenage views:

Kay grew up in a Southern white world of unquestioned segregation. She remembered being disciplined as a young child for addressing African-Americans as "Mrs." or "Sir." But she recalled, "That it didn't make any sense to me. There was that double standard: Be polite to older people, use respect, and say 'Yes, sir' and 'No ma'am,' but not if they're black. Then, when you get to be a teenager and peer pressure takes over, you go along with the crowd. In high school we thought, 'Yeah, they're marching for nothing. It's all a publicity stunt.'" And those were Kay's views at the time of the newspaper article.

"After high school graduation," Kay told me, "I opted not to start college and went to a small Georgia town to train as a reporter at the paper where my father began newswriting in the 1940s. I returned to Albany the next year to work for the *Herald* and take night courses at the University of Georgia Extension Center.

"Then came September 15, 1963. Four little girls were killed in a bombing at the Sixteenth Street Baptist Church in Birmingham, Ala., while they were studying a Sunday school lesson on "The Love that Forgives." One child was eleven. The other three were fourteen, my sister Vicki's age. That's when God took over. My thinking began to change. I had been convinced that stories of the suffering of black people throughout the civil rights movement were grossly exaggerated. If anyone had been hurt they deserved it, I had thought, because they were communists or agitators or ruffians seeking an improper control of things.

"But Denise McNair, Addie Mae Collins, Carol Robertson, and Cynthia Wesley were none of those. They were young girls in church. Suddenly my world made no sense. I searched for answers to the hurt and anger I felt because of their deaths. It would take another year before what I have described as my 'redemption-conversion into a real person' was complete.

"For the next thirty-three years of my life, I wanted to find you, Gloria, and ask your forgiveness. My upbringing hampered that search. I didn't know a single black person in Albany. But I came to know and love many in other places, particularly after my affiliation with the Lutheran church in 1979 and service in synod and churchwide communications from 1985 to 1993."

Kay went to work as a reporter for the Atlanta *Journal-Constitution* in 1996 and then met Alton. When he mentioned that he was from Albany, Kay said, "Alton, you have to help me find somebody."

"Sure, I know Gloria. We're lifelong friends. She is right here in Atlanta, serving Shaw Temple A.M.E. Zion Church as the Rev. Gloria Ward Wright."

Kay and I have become loving friends. She now explains, "For thirty-five years, my sin against a whole race of God's people had had a name: Gloria Ward. She was the only person I could identify whom I had hurt by what I said publicly in 1962. Loving Gloria and being loved in return has been an experience of 'freedom in the gospel' that I truly cannot describe. But I do know that my message to the world must deepen and expand with Gloria beside me. We can multiply this reconciliation a million fold."

7

Response to Dr. Martin Luther King, Jr.'s Speech Forty-three Years Later

"Therefore, my beloved brethren, be ye steadfast, unmovable, always abounding in the work of the Lord, forasmuch as ye know that your labor is not in vain in the Lord." . . . I Corinthians 15:58 (KJV)

"I have a dream that my four little children will one day live in a nation that will not be judged by the color of their skin but by the content of their character."
—Reverend Dr. Martin Luther King, Jr.
August 28, 1963

One night as I found myself preparing to write another chapter of this book, God spoke to my heart. I had no clue as to what I should write next. But I had Dr. Martin Luther King, Jr.'s "I Have Dream Speech" in my hands. Suddenly I heard God answer my question with a question. God said to me, "What is it that you have in your hand? Write a response to Dr. King's speech." This was one part of the book that God made clear to me that I should include.

Let's start with some historical background: Abraham Lincoln issued the Emancipation Proclamation, freeing slaves, in 1862. A century later, President Lyndon Johnson completed the work initiated President John F. Kennedy by signing the Civil Rights Act that banned racial discrimination. The 1964 Civil Rights Act was passed to guarantee the rights of citizens of United States of America, specifically African-Americans, relative to the Thirteenth and Fourteenth Amendments of the United States Constitution. [See *Appendix* for summary of the Civil Rights Act of 1964.]

Although it has been 144 years, African-Americans whose labor helped to build this county are still faced with racial prejudice, discrimination, and second-class citizenship. Now that our nation has become more diverse, African-Americans still find themselves in the position of remaining behind the masses, still last, and still left out. Not only do we, as African-Americans find ourselves feeling alienated in our own country, but we find ourselves having to fight with the very judiciary system that is meant to protect our rights. We can no longer depend on affirmative action, for the action does not always help to protect our rights.

The Lincoln Memorial, 1963

One of the deepest pains of my life came in 1963 when I wanted to join the March on Washington. My mother's words caused an open wound in my spirit when she said, "Gloria, I let you go to Birmingham, Alabama, but you cannot go and join no march on Washington. You could fall out in that crowd, or you could get killed."

My mother was referring to a Southern Christian Leadership Conference (SCLC) meeting in Birmingham that I had attended as a youth speaker. After Dr. King learned of my being arrested and jailed four times in the Albany Movement, he had the Rev. Wyatt Tee Walker write me an invitation to speak at the SCLC conference in Birmingham. Because of the newspaper article about Kay and me, I had become something of a symbol of young black participants in the movement.

The morning we arrived in Birmingham, some of the other youth and I stood on a balcony of the Gaston Hotel and scanned the small crowd below. We played a game of trying to identify one ministerial leader from another as they laughed and talked in the parking lot. I recognized the faces of most of the leaders. Suddenly, I identified Dr. King. I was so excited to see him up close. I had not seen him since his speech at my home church, Mt. Zion Baptist. He was my role model. As young people, it was difficult for us to be in the presence of a man of Dr. King's stature and refrain from getting his autograph or trying to shake his hand.

I went to the stairs, thought for a minute, and leaned over. The others did the same and we all called out, "Good morning!"

Now we had the attention of the ministerial leaders. They looked up and spoke to us. Here was my chance and I took it. I looked directly at Dr. King and said, "Hello!"

"Hello, and what is your name?" he responded.

"My name is Gloria Ward." And with a touch of teenage sassiness, I asked, "What is your name?"—as if I didn't already know.

"My name is Martin King."

After he smiled and spoke to me, I never forgot the look on his face. His smile seemed to say, "This young girl knows who I am. Who does she think she's kidding?"

Yes, I knew who Dr. King was and I was familiar with many other civil rights leaders. However, today it seems to be a little different. Today's young people find it difficult or impossible to identify civil rights leaders. (I will say more about that in Chapter 10.)

When my mother put her foot down and wouldn't let me go to the 1963 Washington March, it seemed as though a spear had pierced my heart. I begged and pleaded with her to no avail. I wanted to go to my room and lock myself up, but I shared only a tiny space with my sisters.

When Dr. King and thousands of freedom fighters and supporters stood on the steps of the Lincoln Memorial on August 28, 1963, they had a purpose in mind. I wanted to attend so badly that my heart still aches more than forty years later. But my very strong mother, who had allowed me to go to jail four times, "put her foot down," as we sometimes say in the South.

Yes, it was quite a day. I watched the action on television as my heart crumbled because I wasn't there with the many friends and classmates with whom I had marched and shared jail cells. The demonstration was one of the first events broadcast around the world via Telstar, a newly launched communications satellite. The three major television networks spent over $300,000 to broadcast the event. CBS even cancelled its afternoon soap operas to cover the speeches for three straight hours.

More than 200,000 demonstrators gathered at the Lincoln Memorial, along the Reflecting Pool, and in front of the Washington Monument to take part in the "March on Washington for Jobs and Freedom," as it was officially called. The march brought widespread attention to the struggle for civil rights. Soon after the march, Dr. King and other leaders met with President Kennedy and Vice President Johnson at the White House. Kennedy told them that he intended to throw his full weight behind civil rights legislation.

Dr. King's chief aide, Rev. Ralph Abernathy, later wrote, "The March on Washington established visibility in this nation. It showed the struggle was nearing a close, that people were coming together, that all the organizations could stand together. It made it clear that we did not have to use violence to achieve the goals which we were seeking."

Presenters and performers that day included Marian Anderson, Joan Baez, Bob Dylan, John Lewis, Odetta, Peter, Paul, and Mary, Paul Newman, A. Philip Randolph, Walter Reuther, Bayard Rustin, Roy Wilkins, and Whitney Young, Jr. But the highlight was Dr. King's closing speech, "I Have A Dream." As he explained, the reason for a massive rally at the Lincoln Memorial was to "dramatize the appalling conditions" in our nation. He said the reason for going to the nation's capital was, in a sense, "to cash a check." He believed that the signers of the Declaration of Independence also "signed a promissory note to which every American was heir."

I have always thought that once an individual signed a promissory note, he or she was held liable or accountable. It seems to me that when one cannot produce results after signing such a document, then that person has forfeited the transaction. Usually when that happens, consequences do follow. I believe, as Dr. King did, that this promissory note should have guaranteed the same rights that were promised in the Declaration of Independence, those rights of life, of liberty and of the pursuit of happiness. People of color continue to suffer the consequences of the actions of others. As a born-again Christian, I believe in the words of the songwriter: "Red, Yellow, Black or White, we are all precious in His sight."

If one were really to look at what has happen over the years, we can understand why Dr. King said, "America has defaulted on this promissory note insofar as her citizens of color are concerned." I agree with Dr. King. America has really issued the African-American community a bad check. Of course, in our society, when one issues a bad check, one has to make it good or suffer the consequences. Those consequences could consist of paying a fine, making the check good, and paying the service charges. It could mean that you could serve time depending on where you are and who you are.

Since our country is one of much wealth, and we do have sufficient funds, America needs to pay African-Americans reparations. Reparations are due us twice: Once for our forefathers' blood, sweat, and tears. Secondly, we are due reparations for the pain, the suffering, and having been short-changed all of our lives. If America is bankrupt and cannot pay us, then she cannot pay anybody else. We, just as Native Americans, are standing in line for payment for a debt that is long past due.

I believe that Dr. Martin Luther King, Jr. and all who followed him to the nation's capital on that very hot and sunny day in 1963 came to make demands on America. The problem seems to be that, although they were there as collection agents, nobody paid on the overdue account. The African-American account, therefore, is still in arrears. The many thousands who appeared in Washington left for home empty handed. We are still awaiting payment while our government seems to have closed our account. Now our chances have diminished inasmuch as there are others who seek payment as we continue to wait.

Racial discrimination still exists. "Driving while black," still carries penalties for the African-American. Police brutality towards African-Americans ends with an apology, and the list goes on and on. In spite of our constantly being mistreated, our African-American soldiers are good for integration only in Iraq, in Liberia, or in some other foreign land.

Today we continue to seek equal opportunities. Yes, we have learned the value of voter registration. Yes, we have learned to vote for certain political candidates. Nevertheless we still seem to fall short in certain areas. Dr. King was right when he said, "Nineteen-sixty-three is not an end, but a beginning." We seem to start over and over and over again. We must not find ourselves just marking time. As a predominantly Christian society, we are taught that "the battle is not ours, but the Lord's." I say we need to be doers of the Word and "watch and pray."

"Upward and Not Backward"

It seems like just yesterday when we prepared to demonstrate for the mass marches. We were told how crucial it was to remain nonviolent. That is very difficult to do when people are shouting and calling you names and hurling bottles and bricks at you, when you are being pulled and pushed to your limits. Mahatma Gandhi of India and Dr. King taught a beautiful lesson of nonviolence. However, there were white folk who took advantage of our nonviolent posture. Some African-Americans were beaten, some lost limbs, and some even lost their lives.

Others criticized the idea of nonviolence. Some militants felt that nonviolence was not the answer. Some felt that more could be accomplished by fighting those who were oppressing us. Among the freedom riders, some whites fought injustices; there were those who marched in the demonstrations, who sang the songs of freedom, who chanted the slogans of confidence as we continued "marching up to freedom land." Yes, we were destined to be free. God was ever present with us and with the one who was chosen, "the drum major for justice."

Dr. King desired that we, as a people, "march upward and not backward." He believed that we should never be "satisfied with mediocrity." As long as we were deprived of our voting rights, as long as we were denied the right to public accommodations, we had to forge ahead and never give up and never give out.

In our struggle for civil rights, our human rights, many youths sacrificed their lives and their families' lives to assist us in the struggle for justice and equality. Dr. King reminded us then, as his dream constantly reminds us today, that we must maintain our dignity and remain disciplined. He taught us, "We cannot walk alone."

On that summer day in the nation's capital, Dr. King, the "drum major for justice," said that he was aware that many of those present had suffered trials and tribulations. Some had just been released from jail cells haunted with the scars of brutality and reminders of suffering and persecution. Nevertheless, he reminded us as a people to never give up. When Dr. King was once asked about being satisfied, he said he believed that we should never be satisfied "until justice rolls down like waters and righteousness like a mighty stream."

About half way through Dr. King's speech, he challenged his attentive audience to go back to their respective places of abode, in the South, to the states of Mississippi, Georgia, and Louisiana. He described some of the other places that they must return to outside the South, such as "the slums and the ghettos of the cities in the North." I believe he really wanted the people to return with expectations, with hope. He wanted them to return with courage, expecting a miracle. He offered encouragement by saying to the people, "Let us not wallow in the valley of despair."

Dr. King reminded his audience that, in spite of the negatives, the difficulties, and the moments of frustration, he still had a dream. This was not just a personal dream that he had, but he said that it was deeply rooted in the American dream. He expressed that in his dream our nation, "America, the Beautiful," would take a stand. He asked our nation to "rise up and live out the true meaning of its creed." Then he eloquently, with anointing resonance, began to recite his take on the Declaration of Independence, including the phrase "All men are created equal."

He stated that one day in the red clay hills of Georgia, "former slaves and their sons, the former slave owners, and their sons would share fellowship, would sit together at the table of brotherhood." In his dream, he saw the state of Mississippi—so feared by travelers and known for many acts of physical violence toward African-Americans—being transformed to an "oasis of freedom and justice." Was this possible? Many travel to Mississippi today and enjoy this beautiful state. Only those who live there can attest to the transformations of this southern state.

Dr. King envisioned his four children, Yolanda, Martin III, Dexter, and Bernice, being treated with respect because their character warranted it. He dreamed of their living in a nation that would not disrespect them because of their skin color. Dr. King's offspring have probably suffered many prejudices, like most African-Americans. One cannot really know what his children, who are now adults, have endured except them and their mother. However, based on looking from the outside, I can see that Dr. King's dream has come to fruition. His four children seem to be respected, and not judged "by the color of their skin but by the content of their character." They appear to be self-sufficient. Their mother, Coretta Scott King, nurtured them to be beautiful, articulate, educated, and to lead lives that enhance society.

Transformation

As Dr. King described his dream, he alluded that although Alabama Governor George Wallace was opposed to desegregation and made statements regarding his feelings of racism, Dr. King felt that Alabama would one day be transformed. He envisioned that children, black and white, would be able to hold hands as sisters and brothers. As he continued to describe his dream, Dr. King quoted Isaiah, 40:4:

"I have a dream that one day every valley will be exalted, every hill and mountain shall be made low, the rough places will be made plain, and the crooked places will be made straight, and the glory of the Lord shall be revealed, and flesh shall see it together."

Dr. King stated, "This is our hope. This is the faith which I return to the South." He declared that hope can be found through our faith. With this faith we can change the discord and disharmony into "a beautiful symphony of brotherhood." He continued by saying that, with this same faith, we can do incredible things, such as working, praying, and struggling together, and be able "to go to jail together, to stand up for freedom together, knowing that we will be free one day."

It seemed to me that God then whispered into Dr. King's ear the words to the song, "My Country 'Tis Of Thee:"

"This will be the day when all of God's children will be able to say with a new meaning, 'My country 'tis of thee, sweet land of liberty, of thee I sing. Land where my fathers died, land of the pilgrim's pride, from every mountainside, let freedom ring.'"

Dr. King made known if America was to become a great nation, the lyrics to the song must be true. So if this is to be true . . .

"So let freedom ring from the prodigious hilltops of New Hampshire.
Let freedom ring from the mighty mountains of New York.
Let freedom ring from the heightening Alleghenies of Pennsylvania!
Let freedom ring from the snowcapped Rockies of Colorado!
Let freedom ring from the curvaceous peaks of California!
But not only that: Let freedom ring from Stone Mountain of Georgia!

Let freedom ring from Lookout Mountain of Tennessee!
Let freedom ring from every hill and every molehill of Mississippi.
From every mountainside, let freedom ring."

The mountains that Dr. King included in his speech are representative of where he saw freedom ringing: from the east coast to the west coast, to the North, and to the South. These four corners of this nation must hear freedom ring. No part of this nation can be excluded.

Why did Dr. King say "let freedom ring" in all these places? He must have known deep down in his spirit that, when we let freedom ring, something is going to happen. He did not say *if* freedom rings. Rather, *when* we let freedom ring, something happens. You may ask, "What happens when freedom rings?" When we let freedom ring from the villages, from the hamlets, from the states, and from the cities, "we will be able to speed up that day when all of God's children, black men and white men, Jews and Gentiles, Protestants and Catholics will be able to join hands and sing in the words of the old Negro spiritual, 'Free at Last! Free at last! Thank God Almighty, we are free at last.'"

At the conclusion of his speech, I noticed that the sound of Dr. King's voice became clearer and stronger. The anointing was on his powerful voice as he delivered this thunderous speech. He spoke with such conviction and with such power. Throughout the world, the "I Have a Dream" speech has been a source of inspiration to me and to millions.

*   *   *

I was finishing this book when Coretta Scott King exchanged time for eternity. She died at age 78 on her son Dexter's birthday, January 31, 2006. She had carried on her husband's legacy for thirty-eight years. Hopefully, the offspring of Martin Luther King, Jr., and Coretta Scott King will continue to carry the legacy of both parents with dignity and pride.

Mrs. King's six-hour funeral service was attended by approximately 15,000 people, including four U.S. presidents, three governors, three planeloads of Congress members, and countless celebrities, singers, and civil rights leaders. The previous day and night, her body had laid in state in Georgia's Capitol Rotunda. That fact was remarkable because the same honor had been denied her husband when he was assassinated in 1968. And that says something about how much of his dream has been fulfilled.

With thousands of others, my son Byron and I paid our respects to Mrs. King. I will let Byron describe it here:

"On February 4, 2006, I stood in line with my mother waiting to view the remains of Mrs. Coretta Scott King at the Georgia State Capitol. It was a historical moment inasmuch as Mrs. King was the very first African-American (and first woman) to lie in state at the state capitol. Hundreds of people patiently waited as we stood in line. Truly, I learned the meaning of being at "the back of the line." That night I understood first hand how important it is, and how hard it can be, to make it to the front of a line. I believe it was the hard work of Dr. King, my mom, and so many others like them that made a positive difference in the lives of all people, especially people of color. As blacks, we have moved from the back of the line and are achieving much success in today's society. If it had not been for those who fought hard for our rights during the civil rights movement, we could have very well been in the back of the line even today."

—Byron Ward Wright

8

Where Have All The Leaders Gone?

"Have not I commanded thee? Be strong and of good courage; be not afraid, neither be thou dismayed: for the Lord thy God is with thee whithersoever thou goest." . . . Joshua 1:9 (KJV)

As a student who marched and participated in mass demonstrations, I was accustomed to being around leaders, such as lawyers, doctors, businessmen, and civil rights leaders. It was exciting to be in the midst of leaders—"hanging around grown people," as the older people say.

I respected and looked up to older people. Even as a young person, I believe that I wanted to be older. Many of my friends at the time were two grades ahead of me. I wanted to be up front, too, but I knew where my place was. There is nothing wrong, of course, with fantasizing about where I wanted to be. You see, the Bible tells us that our words have power. When we speak positively, things begin to happen. I just believe that there is power also in believing. Therefore, we can speak many things into existence. My thinking positively no doubt helped me to succeed in life to become a leader today.

It is interesting to me that, by God's grace, I have come from the back of the line as a student to the front of the line as teacher, as pastor, as motivational speaker, and as an Ambassador of Peace. I have done this by getting an education, by becoming a teacher, by becoming a international servant of God.

I am happy that I had the opportunity to make a difference in our hometown of Albany, Georgia. The older leaders were up front ahead of us, leading the way. Somebody had to lead, and somebody had to follow in order to make a difference. Although Dr. William G. Anderson, Rev. Samuel Wells, Rev. Charles Sherrod, Dr. Martin Luther King, Jr., Elijah "Peter Rabbit" Harris, and many others led us through the streets of Albany, we all had a desire to be free, regardless of our ages. We had a desire to participate as we marched, to protest the injustices and the segregationist practices throughout the city.

As we marched through the streets of Albany to City Hall, some of us were without placards. Nevertheless, we had a song in our hearts. We sang many freedom songs that gave us much hope and courage. Freedom songs made our walk just that powerful. I can still hear Chief Pritchett saying, "You must disburse or you will be arrested." I can still see Mr. A.C. Searles walking up and down on the sideline with a notepad preparing for the upcoming issue of the *Southwest Georgian*, which we called the "black paper." I can still see Mr. Benjamin Cockeran taking pictures for posterity. Even though we demonstrators were serious about what we were doing for humanity, the white racists were serious about making trouble for us, calling us names, hurling rocks at us. Nevertheless, it was worth every mile that we walked and then some.

Many of the civil rights activists have become older. Some have gone on to glory. My Native American friend, Bishop Margie de la Rosa, says it another way. She would say that some have "crossed over to the other side." Nevertheless, those like me are still here. Others may not be the leaders who were at the front of the line during the 1960s. However, they are leaders now in their own right. After forty years have passed, I wonder: Where are the youth who marched with me in those mass demonstrations? This is such a mystery that some have said to me, "Why not have a reunion celebration?"

I wish that I could take the time to find the hundreds of high school and college students who marched in the mass demonstrations of the Albany Movement. I do wonder if those who marched told their children and grandchildren about our struggles. I would be curious to know whether their children and grandchildren were interested in the least.

My real challenge is to present and dedicate this book to those who marched with me and to their children and their children's children. Their children and grandchildren may or may not know of their parents' sacrifices. It is a must! The story must be told. I must tell it to my son and to his children while I am able to recall the history.

This idea of relating the story of the Albany Movement to today's youth reminds me of how many of the "slave stories" seem so remote. Many slaves never told their stories. Even fewer wrote them down because slaves were forbidden to learn to read and write. Therefore, society had to depend on the white man's version as to what happened back in the day.

Those Who Make Things Happen . . .

For more than twenty-four years I taught high school classes in American history, black studies, psychology, and world history. Some students were very interested in classes that addressed the 1960s civil rights events. Conversely, many did not know what happened then and—surprisingly to me—did not have an interest in what happened or why. No wonder someone coined the quotation, "There are those who make things happen, those who watch things happen, and those who wonder what happened."

The writing of this book became almost an obsession for me—not because I wanted to be in some "light of popularity," but because it is my desire to teach or to mentor. We must prepare those who will one day lead us. How can our youth lead us if they don't know where we stopped leading? One day our generation will fade away and die just as the older, prominent civil rights leaders have begun to pass away. What have we told them? What do they know about our fears, our concerns, our hopes, and our dreams for them? What is our legacy?

Yes, Dr. Martin Luther King's dream will forever be remembered. Jesse Jackson gave us hope as he reminded us to "keep hope alive." But, we must teach our youth to bring us a new zeal, a new message of hope, and dreams that come out of that beautiful and powerful, "I Have a Dream Speech" that Dr. King spoke so eloquently in our nation's capital in 1963.

Our youth need direction and purpose. They need to be aware of their past, take charge of the present, and move forward towards the future with a righteous boldness that comes from knowing who you are. Our youth must be challenged to advance with determination, conviction, and pride.

Because of their forefathers and foremothers' sacrifices and contributions, our youth must launch ahead to leave a powerful legacy for their own children and generations yet unborn. Our youth must never be ashamed of our nonviolent tactics that brought us through the civil rights era. Had it not been for the nonviolent methods that Dr. King borrowed from Mahatma Gandhi and taught us to use, we may have had another Civil War.

Our youth now enjoy many things that were denied us at their age. We could not enjoy the movies on the main level of the theaters as today's youth enjoy at Magic Johnson Theaters in Atlanta. We had to sit in the balconies. Restaurants like Paschal's in Atlanta were not available to us as they are today. We had to sit in the back or in a room near the kitchen. Or we could not sit at all, but had to buy our food at a back window for take-out. Today there are hundreds of black-owned restaurants and movie theaters all over this country. White-owned restaurants and movie theaters now compete for our dollars. We have a choice. This is why it is so important that our businesses are superior because we do have a choice now.

Many people have paved the way for us today, just as the slaves paved the way for our grandparents and great-grandparents back in the day.

As a member of the historic African Methodist Episcopal Zion Church (AMEZ), I am reminded of the sacrifices of my forefathers and foremothers. I think of the Zionites, such as Harriet Tubman, Sojourner Truth, Frederick Douglass, and many others, who have paved the way for my heritage.

As a minister and pastor, I give God praise and a special tribute to Bishop James Walker Hood (AMEZ) who ordained Mrs. Julia A. Foote, a conference missionary as a deacon at the Seventy-Third Session of the New York Annual Conference on May 20, 1894, at Poughkeepsie, New York. In 1895, Mrs. Mary J. Small, the wife of Bishop John B. Small, was ordained a deacon at the Sixty-Seventh Session of the Philadelphia and

Baltimore Conference. Other female ministers and I are standing on the shoulders of the Reverend Mrs. Small, "the first woman of Methodism," ordained an elder in 1898 by Bishop Charles Calvin Petty.

Was The Albany Movement a Failure?

Situated in Dougherty County, southwest Georgia, near the Florida and Alabama lines, Albany seemed so far away from Macon and Atlanta when I was a youth. It is a town that I felt always had great potential in the 1960's. As a matter of fact, Albany has potential even today.

Albany's role in the civil rights movement began in the fall of 1961 with the goal of desegregating the whole community. The Albany Movement lasted less than a year, until the end of the summer of 1962. During that brief span, more than 1,000 of us were jailed for participating in mass demonstrations against segregation.

Only a few local leaders were in favor of asking Dr. King to come to Albany. Others thought that he would draw too much attention to Albany. Dr. William Anderson, the president of the Albany Movement, and Mrs. Goldie Jackson, a friend of our family, were responsible for inviting Dr. King.

In December, 1961, Dr. King spoke at a mass meeting, marched with us, was arrested, and jailed along with other leaders like Rev. Ralph Abernathy. People from outside Albany, especially young Student Nonviolent Coordinating Committee (SNCC) workers, came to Albany to conduct a voter registration drive and to challenge segregationist policies. Even Jackie Robinson came to Albany. But as fast as supporters, interfaith ministers, and the media came, it seemed their exit was just as fast.

Unlike some other Southern white police officials, Albany Police Chief Pritchett wanted to avoid violent confrontation with demonstrators because he believed that violence would only invite federal intervention. He told his police officers to avoid brutality. The police were supposed to arrest us and put us in jail until someone bailed us out. Chief Pritchett knew that Dr. King's involvement would draw large numbers of protestors so he arranged with surrounding counties to hold demonstators in their jails whenever the Albany jail filled up.

By the end of the summer of 1962, historians write, Dr. King ran out of willing demonstrators before Chief Pritchett ran out of jail space. That August, Dr. King was arrested again but was let go. He decided that the Albany Movement had fallen short of its goal, that major change in segregationist policies hadn't been achieved. But he and other leaders learned lessons in Albany that they carried on to Birmingham and other Southern cities. After Albany, people in other Georgia towns like Americus and Moultrie were inspired to march and sing and go to jail to challenge segregation.

Not long after the mass demonstrations discontinued and after assessments from the news media, the critics, Chief Pritchett, Dr. King, and others, the Albany Movement was declared a failure. Maybe it did fail from some other people's perspectives. I don't think the Albany Movement was a failure. When I consider all of the good that came about as a result of the Albany Movement, I say that Albany is far better than many Albanians realize.

During the past four decades, Albany can be proud of many African-Americans who have served in outstanding leadership positions: Officer Washington Long became the first African-American Chief of Police; John White served as the first black in the Georgia House of Representatives; Sanford D. Bishop currently serves in the U. S. Congress; Rev. Charles Sherrod and Arthur K. Williams, a high school classmate, served as County Commissioners; the late Mrs. Mamie Reese was appointed to serve on the Georgia Parole Board; Walter Judge served as a local judge; Herbert Phipps serves as a judge on Georgia's Superior Court; and Dr. Willie Adams, Jr., an outstanding gynecologist, is currently serving as the first African-American Mayor of Albany. The list goes on and on . . .

Over the years Albany, now known as the "Good Life City," has blossomed into one of the most progressive and productive cities in Georgia. Dr. Willie Adams, Jr., was elected the first African-American mayor of Albany on March 23, 2004. Recently Dr. Adams was quoted on the front page of the *Albany Herald* as having said this about solidarity in my hometown, "We can work together to make Albany beautiful." I do believe if the citizens, blacks and whites, from east Albany to west Albany, and north of Albany to the south of Albany, would remember what my bishop told our beloved Georgia Conference, Albany will continue to flourish. As Bishop Carr said, "Working together works."

I knew many of the keys players of the movement: Dr. W. G. Anderson, Mr. Marion Page, Attorney C. B. King, Mr. Slater King, Reverend Samuel Wells, Mr. Thomas Chatmon, Reverend H. C. Boyd, Dr. Ed Hamilton, Mrs. Goldie Jackson, and others. Many of the key players belonged to my home church, Mt. Zion Baptist Church. Our pastor, the Reverend Dr. E. James Grant, made significant contributions and many of the mass meetings took place at Mt. Zion Baptist Church.

As I look back, I recall many people who marched with me in the mass demonstrations, and respectfully, I acknowledge them today. I pray that they will read this book and recognize how they changed society. Those who made sacrifices for freedom in the Albany Movement are parents and grandparents today of the youth to whom I dedicate this book. I believe it is imperative that our youth know and remember the names of those courageous students who contributed to the success of desegregation in Albany.

I begin this "roll call" with my friends and schoolmates at Monroe High School: Lillian Simmons, Brenda Boone, Lucille Lattimore, Willie Corbett, Emory Harris, Marva Berry, Selena Craig, Emily Poole, Joyce Johnson, Henry Battle, Larry Gibson, Andrew Reid, Alton Moultrie, Joseph Phipps, Willie Butler, Ola Mae Quarterman, (the Rosa Parks of Albany because she refused to give up her seat on a city bus), Juanita White, Barbara Willis, Juanita James, and several that I cannot find nor recall. Many white supporters came to our aid in the Albany Movement. William Hansen, a SNCC worker, was arrested and beaten in jail as he was called a "nigger lover." Two older white women, Elisa Paschal and Frances Pauley from the Georgia Human Relations Council, came to try to bridge the gap between the white and the black leaderships.

Many students participated in the movement with their family members. Among them were Student Nonviolent Coordinating Committee (SNCC) workers Shirley Gaines, Mamie Ford, Shirley Lawrence, and Joann Christian who convinced their families to march and demonstrate for freedom and justice for all. Other students in the Albany Movement really stood out by going the extra mile in their quest for our freedom. For example: Evelyn Toney, Julian Carswell, and Eddie Wilson were among the many students arrested for putting the Interstate Commerce Commission (ICC) ruling to the test. That ruling mandated that the interstate transportation facilities, such as train stations and bus terminals, were to be desegregated. Albany State College students Blanton Hall and Bertha Gober tested the ICC ruling by going into the bus station, but were arrested for disorderly conduct. Another student who stood out was Annette Jones, Miss Albany State College in 1961. She was crowned queen on the same day as a demonstration at City Hall. When the Albany State College students were brought to trial, more than 300 students from Monroe High School, Carver Junior High School, and Albany State College marched in protest. We marched in the rain and assembled on the steps of City Hall where we sang and prayed.

Five students were tried and convicted. Later, they paid a fine and were released. Of course, help arrived to assist Albany demonstrators in the testing of the ICC ruling. Around December 10, 1961, eight Freedom Riders arrived via train. They were Joan Browning, Norma Collins, Thomas Hayden, Bernard Lee, and Lenora Taitt from Atlanta, Per Laursen from Denmark, and Robert Zellner from Montgomery, Alabama.

Although my picture and my name appeared in newspapers all over the country, no one ever asked me to come back to Albany to speak, other than Mt. Zion Baptist Church and my fortieth reunion for the class of 1963. I submitted materials and papers for the Mt. Zion Museum of Civil Rights, but nothing happened during the reunion of many who returned for a march of tribute. Many don't remember me. I therefore decided to write my own book to express how I began at the back of the line at age at sixteen, trying to make a difference. This is good for all to read, but especially for my only child. I decided not to interview anybody or get anyone to help me with this book, but my plan was to utilize some of the pictures from Cochran Studios through the owner Mr. A.E. Jenkins, Jr. His mother, Mrs. Mary Frances Jenkins, taught me in the seventh grade. I am happy that my wish—to find a group picture with me in it—will come true.

Today I serve as a pastor of Simmons Chapel A.M.E. Zion Church in Lawrenceville, Georgia, and on the board of The Concerned Black Clergy. As I continue to crusade against the ills of society that oppress God's people, especially His people of color, I find that I continue to be driven. We who marched, protested, and shouted, "Down with racism" and "Discrimination must go," were on a mission then, and we are on a mission now.

As a pastor, human rights activist, teacher, wife and parent, I continue to protest with a prophetic voice for the oppressed and the downtrodden. As a board member of the Concerned Black Clergy of Atlanta, I have assisted in championing many causes:

voter registration, homelessness, health, education, juvenile justice infrastructure, the end of landfills in our communities, and many others. Whether I am given credit or not, I still fight the ills of our society and the world.

My reward comes from my Maker, my Creator, my Sustainer, the Author and Finisher of my faith, my Lord and Savior, the One who has brought me through the valley and up many rocky mountains. Still I am "no ways tired." My God has brought me through dangers seen and unseen. My God has brought me full circle from the back of the line to lead with the same pride, the same courage, and the same dignity as when I followed. Thanks be to God for the things that He has done in my life "from the back of the line."

9

Preordained to be Ordained

"Before I formed thee in the belly I knew thee; and before thou camest forth out of the womb I sanctified thee, and I ordained thee a prophet unto the nations." . . .
Jeremiah 1:5 (KJV)

I once heard someone say that teachers, ministers, and morticians are the leaders in the African-American community. I really cannot argue that point. When I was graduated from college, I accepted a position as public school teacher. Eighteen years later, I accepted the call into ministry.

It seems that I was being prepared for this call through out my lifetime. I am often asked, "When did you decide to go into the ministry?" I did not decide to go into the ministry. I was called into the ministry by my Creator. I entered the ministry from the classroom and from the choir loft. At the time, I was teaching full-time and singing in the Gospel Chorus at Shaw Temple A.M.E. Zion Church in Atlanta.

I had been reared as a Baptist, but I became a Methodist after a senior citizen friend, Mrs. Mary Cobb (now deceased), and a friend and neighbor, Patricia Damron Malone, invited me to Shaw Temple A.M.E. Zion Church. Pat went a step further and invited me to a sunrise service one Easter morning at Shaw. Pat's uncle, Wilford Ray, and his wife Ruth encouraged me to join the choir and become a member of the church.

I find it interesting when individuals say that women have no place in ministry. Men and women can be used in the service of mankind. God uses willing vessels. I was told that "some are called, some are sent, and some just went." I do believe that I was called. Since I accepted the call into ministry nineteen years ago, I have prospered and I have been at peace. It is amazing how God will place you some place just for a season and, then, sometimes for a lifetime.

I preached my trial sermon on December 6, 1987, at Shaw Temple A.M.E. Zion Church. As a teacher, my sermon title was "Lessons on Faith." There were procedures to follow in order to move up in ministry. After accepting the call as minister, more responsibilities were added, such as studying an assigned curriculum from the denomination, attending constant meetings, attending seminary, paying ministerial dues, and then pastoring a church. I could not have asked for that, nor could I have done it without Dan, my devoted husband.

The process of moving up in ministry began by studying and assisting my pastor and presiding elder, the late Dr. John Wesley Smith, in the pulpit. I was also in school part-time, studying for my master's degree at the Interdenominational Theological Seminary, teaching high school, and being a wife and mother. Within two years, Bishop Cecil Bishop asked me at the Annual Conference about taking a church. I explained to him that I had a husband, a seven-year-old son, and a full-time teaching job.

Before the conference, my husband had told me, "If you are asked, do not take a church." Well, on the last day of the conference, preachers were lined up to receive their appointments. We were about to be sent to pastor and to preach the gospel. I did not mind having a church at all because I love God and God's people. I am not a shy person. For years, I had been standing and speaking before students all day long. Public speaking had never been a problem for me, so I said to God, "Bring it on!"

But my husband had said, "Do not take a church," so I was in a bind. Some of the ministers had told me that, when you are given an assignment from the bishop on the last day of conference, you are to say simply, "Thank you, Bishop." Then you are expected to go to your church on the following Sunday.

When it came time for the bishop to announce ministerial appointments, each pastor's name would be called. We were to shake the bishop's hand and move on. I really wasn't sure if I would get a church this time. I was strapped with school, work, and family. I knew what the Bible says about being anxious for nothing, but knowing what my husband had said, I became quite anxious.

Most of the ministers' names had been called. Suddenly Bishop Cecil Bishop called out my name, "Sister Gloria Ward Wright." (I was *Sister* because I had not yet been ordained to merit the title of Reverend.) The bishop then called out the names of two churches, Thomas Chapel A.M.E. Zion Church in Lyerly, Georgia, and Mt. Zion A.M.E. Zion Church in Coosa, Georgia. I began to sweat under my robe. I felt as though I would faint. "Oh, my goodness, not one, but two churches. Now what do I do? What will I tell Dan?"

After the conference ended, I spoke to no one. I got into my car to drive home. Thirty minutes later I stopped at a service station. I realized that I was still wearing my clergy robe. I took off my robe, filled my car with gas, and headed home.

Later that night my husband called from California. "Honey, how did the conference go?"

"It went quite well," I answered.

"Tell me, did you get a church?"

"No, Dan, I didn't get a church." I could hear his little sigh of relief over the telephone. He was about to say something when I cut in and said, "Excuse me, Honey, I did not get a church. I was given two churches." Since that conversation, life has never been the same.

Up the Mountain

I served approximately eighteen months at Thomas Chapel A.M.E. Zion Church and about twelve months at Mt. Zion. To get to these rural churches, up in the mountains near the Tennessee border, I drove long, winding roads in my old beat-up Ford Fairlane with four "maypops," slick tires with very little tread.

I didn't travel alone because angels escorted us for the ninety-nine mile, one-way trip. Byron, strapped in his safety gear in the back seat of the car, encouraged me with his singing of "Father Abraham Had Many Sons, Many Sons Had Father Abraham." Most children who go to church know the song. My husband often rode with us to my assigned churches. When Dan did not go with us, I loaded up the car with friends. Sometimes a caravan followed us to the church. At Thomas Chapel, only a few people came to church, but God was with us at all times. There were about twenty members, but I preached as though there were thousands seated before me. On the way home after church, we would stop in Rome, Georgia, to have dinner as a family.

After twelve months at Mt. Zion, I had a very serious fall in the classroom and injured my back. The injury caused me to retire from teaching prematurely. I gave up Mt. Zion. A few months later, I had to give up Thomas Chapel as well because the long drive was causing me a lot of back pain.

[The injury affects me even today, but *through physical therapy, periodic injections for pain, and chiropractic care, I am able to do what I do. Had it not been for God sending me miraculous chiropractic care from Dr. Tony Denmark and Dr. Jay DiVagno, I would have had a most difficult time making it physically. More importantly, "if it had not been for the Lord on my side," I would not have made it at all. Before I go on pilgrimages, my doctor gives me injections for pain that last for about three months. By God's Grace, my prayers, my* faith, and my determination, I am able to persevere. But I have to practice to remain upbeat. People who know me know that I don't care for negative talk. For example, I answer the telephone with the expression, "Praise the Lord" instead of "Hello" because praising God is like breathing for me. I don't stay in the company of negative people very long because I feel the need to glorify God and to edify the people of God. I often find myself looking for something positive to say to and about the people that I meet and to people that I know. By staying positive-minded, by meeting new people, by experiencing new people and new places, my life is healthier and happier.]

After the fall in the classroom and resigning from Mt. Zion and Thomas Chapel, I returned to Shaw Temple, my home church in the A.M.E. Zion denomination. For six years, I was an associate at Shaw where the Rev. Dr. John Wesley Smith was pastor once again. My back injury improved after I came off the road. But Sunday after Sunday many friends and church members would ask me when I was going to branch out and start my own church. My answer was simply, "I will move from here when God calls me by my name to leave."

I was ordained a deacon in the African Methodist Episcopal Zion Church by Bishop Cecil Bishop in 1989. This ordination afforded me the opportunity to serve as pastor and to serve communion. However, without elder's ordination, I had to get a friend and colleague, Dr. N'dugu T'fori-atta, to bless the bread and wine. I preached my trial sermon entitled, "Holding On To The Master Teacher of Faith," at Shaw Temple A.M.E. Zion Church, the mother church of the Georgia Conference, and served as an associate with Dr. Smith and then the Rev. Dr. Louis Hunter respectively.

In October 1993, with the recommendation of Dr. Louis Hunter, Sr., (now Bishop Hunter) I was ordained an elder by my newly elected bishop, Bishop George Battle at Mt. Zion A.M.E. Zion Church in Augusta, Georgia. I believe that I was one of the first ministers and one of the first females that he ordained following his election. Bishop Joseph Johnson and Bishop Clarence Carr were among a host of bishops elected at the Hilton Hotel in Atlanta when Shaw Temple was the host church for that General Conference. Dr. Smith was the Host Pastor and Host Presiding Elder. After the General Conference, Dr. Smith was moved on to serve in Hackensack, New Jersey. The newly elected bishop, Bishop Battle, became my bishop. He served to 1996 when my newly assigned bishop came in the person of Bishop Joseph Johnson.

Remember my famous last words, "I will move from here when God calls me by my name"? Well, it happened. I was called by name to go to Simmons Chapel A.M.E. Zion Church in Lawrenceville as an interim pastor until a replacement could be found. I had preached at that little church previously. One earlier Sunday as I drove to the church as the guest preacher, I spoke into my spirit these words, "This is a breeze. If I had this church, I could handle this thirty-eight miles—one way!" Wow! Be careful what you speak, God is listening.

After serving as interim pastor for about one month, I went to our annual conference in 1998. Bishop Joseph Johnson asked me if I would remain as the pastor of Simmons Chapel. Indeed, I was very happy to accept this new challenge. There were only three persons at the church. When I arrived at the church, I was met by Brother Henry A. Brown in the parking lot. I told him I was the new pastor of Simmons Chapel. He said, "You may be the pastor, but ain't no members here, and ain't no money here either." I replied to Brother Brown, "The Lord has sent me here to work. I've come to serve the Lord and His people."

Simmons Chapel is a small, cinderblock building in the middle of downtown Lawrenceville near the Justice Center. The former pastor had left to begin a new ministry and thirty-five members went with him. I had the remaining three. One member, the oldest member of the church, was in the nursing home. I knew that my work was cut out for me.

When I drove the thirty-eight miles to Simmons Chapel that first Sunday, I had no key to enter the building. It was Communion Sunday, and the bread and wine were inside under lock and key. There I was, the new pastor standing in the parking lot without a key to the church. I called one of the Simmons Chapel trustees to come and unlock the door for us.

A few visitors showed up and we waited in the parking lot. After thinking prayerfully for a few minutes, I announced that we would have church right there. Yes, we had a spirit-filled time in the parking lot. Just before I was about to preach the sermon, the trustee drove up with the key to open the church doors, and we entered the church to complete the service.

Where Miracles Happen

That Sunday was the beginning of the longest time that I have ever pastored a church. In October, 2006, I began my eighth year as pastor of a church that I named "The Little Church Where Miracles Happen." The reason for the name was simple. The members and others were speculating that the church was going to be closed. But I felt that this was God's house, and I would do everything in my power to keep it open.

After much prayer, I decided that the only way that this church would survive was to make it look like a church. I looked through the sanctuary and noticed that there was no altar in this Methodist church. I asked Brother Brown why was there no altar. He said one of the previous pastors had said that space should be left at the front of this small church for the casket.

I could not hold my peace. I shouted, "Whose casket?"

"Mrs. Daisy King and I are the oldest," he said. "I guess the pastor thought that one of us would die soon."

"We are getting an altar," I said, "because (excuse my ebonics) ain't nobody gonna die."

I called my brother Ernest, a contractor in Albany, and asked him to come to Lawrenceville, which is about 200 miles from Albany. I told him that this little building needs to look like a church.

"I am reminded of the expression that if it walks like a duck, acts like a duck, quacks like a duck, then it must be a duck," I said, to prove a point. We tried with all our might to make Simmons Chapel look and act like a church.

I designed a steeple to be placed on the church, and Ernest built it to my specifications. Then we needed an altar. Ernest and my other brother Carl put their heads together to come up with an altar. A friend of the family, Mrs. Elizabeth Robinson, made cushions for the altar. After the steeple and the altar were completed, visitors started coming. My friends and family came to the church from Atlanta. They made contributions, helped with music, and helped with cleaning the church. We held special programs. The Progressive Club, of which my husband and I are members, donated an air-conditioner. Another family friend, Mr. Charles Tunstall, rewired the church to accommodate increased wattage for the air conditioner. Later we added a ramp for the handicapped. God was blessing us with so many miracles. Each time that we gave God the credit, God blessed us even the more.

To show just how God blessed us, I want to acknowledge the contributions made to "the little church where miracles happen" (and I don't dare call individual names). There were monetary contributions on Sundays and during special programs. Gifts presented to the church included a regular piano, an electric baby grand piano, a public address system, speakers, two ceiling fans, the first hot water heater, two ceramic sinks, two new gas heaters, a refrigerator, a cross for the altar, puppets for the children's church and our puppet ministry, and many more miracles.

As a church family, we paid our financial obligations to the denomination by way of our tithes and offerings. We purchased office furniture for pastor's study and installed the first telephone in the 117-year of the history of the church. Finally, we had a television ministry for about six months, business cards for our members, and a web site (www.littlechurchofmiracles.com) that is very informational, comprehensive, and most attractive.

God allowed our church to flourish by growing from three to sixty members. Many more came to us, stayed for months to a year, and moved on. On Sundays our church is one of the most spirit-filled churches in the nation. Although we can account for only twenty-five members today, we feel that God has truly blessed us beyond our ability to ask.

What does this have to do with this book? Why do I include the history of Simmons Chapel A.M.E. Zion Church in this account of my life and the civil rights movement? I believe that the hard working members who helped me to make Simmons Chapel African Methodist Episcopal Zion Church also helped to make me who I am today. They were with me through the trials and the triumphs. Had they not been with me, I would have remained at the back of the line. Their dedication to God and to their pastor made each one of them a leader at the front of the line.

Churches played a vital role in the civil rights movement. Recently, when I was reading the history of the movement, I ran across the names of many of our bishops. The first bishop of my denomination, the A.M.E. Zion Church, Bishop James Varick set the stage. According to Bishop William J. Walls, author of *The African Methodist Episcopal Zion Church: Reality of the Black Church,* the following words were stated in a proclamation:

"James Varick, the first bishop, won a high place in the history of his country by his unselfish motives, sterling sagacity, and sacrificing leadership. By the example of him and his associates who refused to remain in a condition where people of color worshipped from the gallery, were forced to wait for Holy Communion until white members were served, and where no persons of their race were ordained elders; this race self-enterprise and self-expression in America was begun . . ."

Before I discuss a little more of history of the A.M.E. Zion Church, I want to comment on the quotation in Bishop Wall's book that I believe to be most significant. To me, the people of the church have to come from within the walls of the church and go into the vineyards and tell a dying world about Jesus. After traveling with interfaith groups, I realize that all do not accept Jesus the Christ. Nevertheless, I must tell about my relationship with Jesus and go from there. In Biblical times, Jesus said to the disciples and, yes, He is yet saying to us these same words known as the Great Commission, "Go ye therefore into all the world and teach and preach, baptizing in the name of the Father and of the Son and of the Holy Ghost."

I firmly believe that we who claim to be church-going Christian leaders should worship in the church and out of the church. We should work diligently in the church. Nevertheless, there is a need for ecumenicity. There is need to associate with other persons or other inter-faith groups in the community. I believe that no one denomination should boast about how great its denomination is. You see, when one shares, discusses, and exchanges ideas of ministry, evangelism, and missions, then we can grow.

I believe that every church should have on-going in-service training relative to witnessing, Christian education, missions, and ministerial training. I believe, however, that there is another side to training, and that is to travel to the holy sites listed in the Holy Bible, the Holy Koran, or from whatever is your Holy or Sacred Book.

The best education that I have received was not from classes, books, and videos. The best education that I have been afforded was when I actually went on pilgrimages to the Holy Land with other ethnic groups, to listen to the language, to see the foods that they ate, to watch various groups purchase items for their loved-ones, etc.

To associate with my people of color is the ultimate. Nevertheless, I also want to associate with a mixture of other ethnic groups, persons of other religious persuasions, and people of other cultures, dressed in their native regalia. I remember sharing a conversation with some Native Americans. One Native American man explained that one must not refer to Native American dress as "Indian costumes" because they prefer to be addressed as Native Americans and not Indians. Their clothes are not costumes, but they should be referred to as regalia.

I am happy to know that our deceased bishop Bishop William J. Walls said in his book, *Reality of the Black Church*, that the A.M.E. Zion Church is affiliated with several other ecumenical organizations, such as the Church Women United, The American Bible Society, The National Council of Churches, the World Methodist Council, just to name a few. I am proud that my church affiliates with interfaith organizations and supports their causes and purposes to the fullest extent in the nation and around the world. Representatives among our ministry and laity are continuously sent to multicultural meetings. They participate well in these movements of unity and ecumenicity.

Controversial Leaders

"The ultimate measure of a man," Dr. Martin Luther King, Jr., said, "is not where he stands in moments of comfort and convenience, but where he stands at times of challenge and controversy."

The most controversial leader who impacted my life is Jesus, the Christ, the one who was born of a virgin, born in a stable. The one who was crucified because He claimed to be and is the Messiah, the Anointed One, the Prince of Peace, the King of Kings and Lord of Lords, the One who came to save the world. Jesus was controversial for many reasons. He changed water into wine, made the dumb to talk and the lame to walk. This controversial Jesus fed 5,000 people with a little boy's lunch and healed people on the Sabbath Day.

Because He upset so many with His claims to be God, He was crucified dead and was buried. But just as the Old Testament Scriptures have said to us through the prophets, one day He would rise up on the third day with all power in His hands, the power to do. Yes, Jesus was a most controversial leader. I decided to follow Him a long time ago.

When I was a child we used to say, "You can talk about me as much as you please, but the more you talk, the more I am going to bend my knees." How do we, as Christians, judge others when the Bible says, "Judge ye not . . ."? God wants us to love one another. Anyone can see that everything about Jesus points to love. We must love our neighbors, our enemies, and ourselves. We are all responsible for our work down here on earth. We must give an account for our labor. God speaks to us. I know that God speaks to me. Therefore, what God says to me, He may not say to you. Nevertheless, I respect you for whatever relationship you say that you have with God. Of course, I want the same respect in return.

At age sixteen, I saw Dr. King as a controversial leader because he was accused of womanizing and of associating with communists. Nevertheless, that never stopped me from respecting him, recognizing his strengths, following his lead, and following his dream. I followed Dr. King and other leaders from my parents' house all the way to the jailhouse as we protested the ills of segregation and Jim Crowism.

(The term "Jim Crow" described the laws and customs that maintained the almost total separation of African-Americans from whites in the South. The Jim Crow character was a stereotype of an old black man and was first used in a minstrel show by a white comedian in 1832, but the identity of the original Jim Crow is uncertain.)

We marched peacefully together and were arrested and jailed together, but through it all we brought about changes that made the world a better place in which to live—not perfect, just better. We must continue to fight for justice and equality. We have come along way, but we have a long way, yet, to go. Yes, we shall overcome some day and the truth will set us free.

Someone once said: "Freedom ain't free." Because of controversial people like Dr. King and others, progress has been made in this country from the bus boycotts in Montgomery, Alabama, to the sit-ins at the lunch counters in Greensboro, North Carolina, and from the marches in Albany, Georgia to the March on Washington, D.C.

Several years ago the Rev. Sun Myung Moon, the visionary and founder of the American Clergy Leadership Conference (ACLC), impacted my life through the international and inter-religious organization of ministers. He is another controversial leader, but I believe the fact that Rev. Moon served time for tax evasion does not make his commitment to the human race any less powerful.

The ACLC, which has over 14,000 interfaith ministers, caught my attention because of the organization's strong belief in marriage and family values. I was impressed with the pilgrimages taken to the Middle East to promote peace. Together the three Abrahamic faiths joined hands together to walk the streets of Amman, Jordan, to protest the bombings of the hotels there.

A permit had never been given to Americans to march in Amman's streets. Hundred of interfaith clerics, imams, rabbis, and Christian ministers peacefully marched to each hotel. When we arrived at the hotel, we signed a banner hanging on the wall at the front of the hotel. Together we sang, we prayed, and, yes, together we made a difference. At least we were able to sit down and have peace talks with the clerics when others could not and others did not.

Jesus is the Way, the Truth, and the Life. Jesus promised us through the Holy Scriptures that "greater works would we do." Without a doubt, Jesus Christ is my Lord and Savior. As another writer once said, "I know who I am and whose I am" because I can see good in all people and I can work with all people for the good of mankind.

If I share some of your views that does not mean that I give up my life and hand it over to you. When I work in concert with you to make this world a better place to live, that does not mean that I abandon my faith. My faith becomes stronger when it is being tested.

My travels to the Holy Land represented my personal quest to promote peace even though I traveled with an interfaith group that was founded by a controversial visionary, Rev. Moon. I am no more a Unificationist because I have traveled, read Scriptures, and prayed with Unificationists than he is a Methodist. Some of the most beautiful people whom I have ever encountered were mainly Japanese missionaries from the Unification Church. Others came from other places, but the Japanese missionaries stand out. On our pilgrimages I have shared hotel rooms with a few of them. They are courteous, loving, pleasant, and friendly. If I were to keep it real, I would say that they, more than any other people, have shown me what it means to be a servant.

On a pilgrimage that I made to Israel in May, 2005, it was so hot when we walked to and from the various Holy sites. As I returned from touring and headed for the bus, I was perspiring and thirsty. One of the missionaries was waiting with a cold washcloth to wipe my over-heated, sweaty face. I was so touched by her Christ-like spirit. To me that was analogous to washing my feet.

So many marvelous people in the world are misunderstood. We as Christians look down our noses, so to speak, to judge them. I can go on and on about people of the world. God is going to hold us accountable for how we scorn and reject people. I am not gay, but some in our churches all over the world are gay. If we say that this is not true, then we are in denial. Yes, we are taught to hate sin, but not the sinner. The Bible says that we have all fallen short of the Glory of God. Should we point the finger? I don't think so. We all have some skeletons in our closets. Sometimes those skeletons in our closets have meat on their bones. Therefore, will I stop and say, "Because you are different I cannot counsel you or I cannot communicate with you"? No, I have to counsel or associate with those who are red, yellow, black, white, rich, poor, gay, straight, Republican, or Democrat. Just because my roommate happens to be Republican, that doesn't make me a Republican.

Because I love to visit the Church of Latter Day Saints headquarters in Salt Lake City doesn't make me a member of that church. I believe it is because of my contacts with people of all walks of life that I find myself growing. You see, it is not important that someone can influence me to be like them, but rather others can see me and the light that I bring with me. The light of Jesus illuminates me. We must remember that people take notice of us at all times. Someone once said that we are the only Bible that others may read. The Bible says that we are to be the light of the world. We are to shine so that others can see our good works and glorify God, our Creator. We are the salt of the earth. I learned long ago that salt gives flavor to food. But more importantly, salt preserves. It keeps things from decaying. We must be the salt to keep this world from decaying. We must give light to those who are in darkness. Furthermore, we must be salt to this world to help keep it fresh and pure.

We can be truly free, ultimately, only together . . . black and white, rich and poor, Christian, Muslim, Hindu, Buddhist, and Jew . . . God's dream wants us to be brothers and sisters, wants us to be family.—Archbishop Desmond Tutu, Nobel Laureate

My involvement with the American Clergy Leadership Conference has included several pilgrimages to various areas of Asia and the Middle East, such as Jordan, Israel, and South Korea, as well as to Rome, at my own expense. Because of my experiences with the organization, I have moved closer to the front of the line as a leader. I have prayed with other ministers for the reunification of North and South Korea. I have traced the footsteps of Paul in Rome. I have walked in the footsteps of Jesus, prayed at the Garden of Gethsemane, and read Scriptures in the Upper Room. I have been baptized in the Jordan River. I have looked over the Mount of Olives. I have seen a little of what Moses saw from Mount Nebo and bathed my body in the Dead Sea.

My experiences have been so very much enriched as a result of being in the presence of other ethnic groups, other creeds, and other races and nationalities of people at levels that might not have otherwise been available to me. I thank God for how He has blessed me. I say in the paraphrased words of the songwriter, "Any way you bless me Lord, I will be satisfied."

My God has promised me that He will never leave me or forsake me. Well, I know that some intellect will say, "Don't refer to God as He," but I say that I do understand inclusively. Nevertheless, I love and obey Almighty God, and God answers my prayers whether I say Mother God or God the Father. We Christians get so hung up on every little detail. We need to practice being good Christian role models for generations to come. No wonder our children and youth do not come to stay at our churches. We are entirely too critical, too political, sometimes hypocritical, and we become so holy that we become no earthly good.

In closing out my comments about controversial leaders and Rev. Moon, I say:

"I know who I am and whose I am because I can see good in all people and I can work with all people for the good of mankind and "for the sake of others." If I share some of your views, that does not mean that I give up my life and hand it over to you. When I work in concert with you to make this world a better place in which to live, that does not mean that I abandon my faith. My faith becomes stronger when it is being tested."

The Links Between Teaching and Pastoring

I began this chapter by saying that leaders in African-American communities are often teachers, ministers, and morticians. Well, I've never been a mortician, but I do believe that there has been a great similarity and overlap between teaching and pastoring in my own life. I think my pastoring has been strengthened by my earlier career in the classroom.

During my adult life and throughout my teaching career, I have been very active in fighting causes. I was a hard-working teacher. I was harder on myself, however, always pushing myself to be the best that I could be. I was driven. I was challenged. Everyday when I entered the classroom, I tried to teach something new and exciting. I remember on Fridays after working myself into a frazzle, I would have the students present a current events article, discuss it, and then show on the world map where the event took place.

On some Fridays, I would have the students sit in a circle to hold discussions. One particular discussion came from the students answering this question: "What bugs me?" You would be surprised at what bugs our young people. I dare anyone to try this at home. It does not matter the age, but do try it. This simple question could lead to releasing a lot of tension or getting a lot off of one's chest, as some would say.

Many humorous incidents took place during my teaching career. One in particular happened when a female student did not turn in her homework. I took her aside and tried to intimidate her, very gingerly, into completing her assignment. I said, "Deborah, I am going to call your father if you do not turn in your assignment by the end of the school day."

"Mrs. Wright," she replied, "Call my father if you want, but my Mama wears the pants in our house." This incident taught me a lesson, which is to never to be presumptuous.

Another humorous incident took place one day in late spring during the last period of the day, a hot and stuffy time typical of many sixth period classes. The air conditioning was not working properly. I was reviewing some final examination questions with my students. I noticed that one of my seniors had placed her head on the desk, which was a definite "no no." I asked some students near Belinda to awaken her, but she didn't move.

As I walked toward her, I said, "Belinda, do you know the answer to my question?" But she kept her head down on the desk. A male student with a smirk on his face said, "Mrs. Wright, she said let her sleep on it!" The students laughed so hard, I had to smile. By the time we collected ourselves, the bell rang for dismissal.

A teacher has to be serious, but at times we also enjoy the students' comic relief. For the most part, students know that in order to learn, pass a course, and be successful in school, they have to stay alert, stay focused, and do the work that has been assigned. Some of the best days of my life were spent teaching young men and young ladies, many who, today, are parents and teachers themselves.

So many rewarding things took place during my tenure as a high school history teacher. In retrospect, my only regret is that my travels to various countries came long after I left the classroom. If I had traveled more prior to teaching, I believe that I would have made a much better teacher.

Nevertheless, I won plaques and trophies for my abilities as a teacher. One particular award was the Academic Achievement Incentive Award that was presented to me in social science for the Atlanta Public Schools. I was the only teacher chosen for the whole school system. The best thing about it was that I was the first to win the award because it was the first year the program was initiated. One teacher and one student were selected per discipline, for instance, in mathematics, in science, in English and in my area, social science.

I received another award, sponsored by the Quaker Oats Company, from the National Council of Negro Women (NCNW). I received a beautiful award and a monetary gift of $500. No, I did not save the money. I used it to travel to yet another part of God's beautiful universe. Everybody who knows me knows that I love to travel, not shop like sensible women.

I did not get to compete on the national level for the NCNW award, but I was so grateful to have been recognized locally. On the dais at the Atlanta awards breakfast, I was pleasantly surprised to find myself seated next to Mrs. Coretta Scott King. We exchanged pleasantries. When she discovered that I was a minister in the A. M. E. Zion Church, she commented, "I started out as an AME Zionite."

I smiled and replied, "You had good taste, Mrs. King." She responded with a smile and raised eyebrows. I told her that I had marched as a teenager with her husband in the Albany Movement. She smiled and looked at me as though a light bulb went off, and then inquired, "Have you told my daughter Bernice about this?"

I said, "No, Ma'am, I have not." She spoke as if I had talked to her daughter or met her daughter. So I explained, "I have never had the pleasure of meeting your daughter." I did not get a chance to tell her anything else because the program started and our conversation ended abruptly. Now I often wonder but will never know, why was it important that I would tell Elder Bernice King that I had marched with her father in the Albany Movement when I was sixteen years old?

10

The Way I See It: Commentary on the Past, the Present, and the Future

"Finally, brethren, whatsoever things are true, whatsoever things are honest, whatsoever things are just, whatsoever things are pure, whatsoever things are lovely, whatsoever things are of good report; if there be any virtue, and if there be any praise, think on these things." . . . Philippians 4:8 (KJV)

As a child, I grew up pledging allegiance to the United States' flag. The red, white, and blue "Old Glory" represented the country that I loved and still love so much. It is the most reverenced patriotic symbol for our country. The pledge stated that the flag represented "the republic for which it stands." We were taught that we lived in a nation that was under God, "indivisible, with liberty and justice for all." We recited this pledge every morning before beginning our school day. We prayed and read inspirational quotations. This was the highlight of my day. Although I loved my country, the country did not seem to love me back. I was treated as a second-class citizen just as other brothers and sisters of color were.

Today there are those who want to end the Pledge of Allegiance or remove the phrase "under God." The Supreme Court was to decide. The National Education Association (NEA), one of the nation's most prominent teacher organizations, of which I was a member for years, gave its position on the matter. Less than a week after the Ninth Circuit Court's decision, the NEA Board of Directors voted to support the Pledge of Allegiance. The NEA's position was as follows: "NEA does not believe that the inclusion of the words 'under God' in the Pledge of Allegiance poses a threat to the principle separation of church and state." (*NEA Today*, April, 2004, p. 23) I concur with the NEA Board of Director's position. If the truth were told, we need all of the help that we can get in the public schools. We have been saying the pledge with the phrase, "one nation under God," for decades and we had problems in our schools. I shutter to think what will happen without the phrase "under God."

Today we have additional concerns that are part of traditions that some want to abandon in our schools. For instance, at Christmas time, we sang Christmas carols, held Christmas parties and pageants, made Christmas bulletin boards, and served a Christmas lunch with turkey, dressing, and all the trimmings. We pulled names out of a hat and exchanged gifts. These were some of the best days of my life. And now, once again, we must prepare for another challenge from others who are disgruntled with Christmas being a part of a school year.

How sad this is, for some children only have Christmas dinner with all the trimmings at school, and the once-a-year excitement of Christmas only takes place at school for them.

These same traditions took place when I taught high school for many years. During my son Byron's days in school, he enjoyed the same traditions as his parents had enjoyed. Today everything seems to be changing. Thanks to Madelyn O' Hare, her disciples, and atheists, those who are Christians cannot really celebrate Christmas as we did in the past. I realize that there are students and educators of other faiths in our schools. Since that is the case, maybe we should consider celebrating all the major holidays. Now if you think that this will not work for persons of other religious persuasions, think again.

Consider discontinuing the Christian holidays, the Jewish holidays, and the Islamic holidays. I make no apologies for being a Christian, but I say that people of all faiths take off and enjoy the Christmas holidays with great pleasure. We must learn to celebrate the holidays of others, learn the significance of each holiday, and learn from people who celebrate holidays that we may not celebrate. We are a most diverse population in this country. Our diversity comes with our likes and dislikes, our cultures, our customs, our mores, our faiths, and yes, even, our idiosyncrasies. Let us learn from our diversities. Let us grow from our learning. The more that we learn about each other the less we fear one another.

Another holiday we take without hesitation is Martin Luther King, Jr.'s Birthday. Many people all over this country really do give Dr. King respect by honoring him on his birthday. However, I assure you that those who disliked Dr. King or those who continue to be racists are not begging to go to work on Dr. King's birthday. Consider checking out some of the airlines, some of the golf courses, some of the hotels and/or the resorts on Dr. King's birthday. Must we be reminded that the holiday should be "a day on and not a day off "?

Liberty and Justice for All?

Do we really have liberty and justice for all? One way to find the answer to this question is to research the laws of the past and the present laws of this country. Since this book is dedicated to our youth, a reality check would be to read all about the legislation regarding "No child left behind" and analyze it. Then read the *Atlanta Journal Constitution'* article "Throwing Away the Key" (in Section F of the paper from Sunday, March 28, 2004) written by Martha M. Ezzard. It is a riveting account of how our young black males are being "warehoused" in our Georgia prisons. It speaks of the law that Georgia passed over ten years ago. This law puts our sons and daughters into prison for a minimum of ten years without parole for committing crimes that are considered as one of the seven deadly sins. Our juveniles are sent off to prisons that house adult criminals. Our youth end up serving two sentences, one for the state and one for the adults that are in the prisons. They end up having to fight the system and fight the prisoners. Many are taken advantage of by the older prisoners.

I am not advocating that those who break the law should not be punished. However, I am saying that juveniles should be placed with juveniles to serve their time. Otherwise, if we allow this to continue, we are contributing to the delinquency of minors even further. The statistical reports of our black youth in prison are alarming. I am concerned for our youth. Our youth are at risk!

When we look at the young black population and see those who are in the prisons versus those who are in college, it should give us goose pimples. Our young men are being victimized both on the outside of prisons and on the inside of prisons. When we put them in the lion's den with the hardcore criminals, we are giving permission to abuse our youth physically and emotionally. We read daily about our youth being abused, brutally assaulted, and sodomized. Is this justice? Or is this "just us?"

We must not turn our heads and pretend that these violent acts against our youth are not happening. They will not go away! We must do something for juvenile justice. I remember taking my concerns to the Concerned Black Clergy about the fact that our youth can hardly call home to talk about their concerns. They call home and their parents, oftentimes single mothers, are faced with outrageous telephone bills. These bills range in the hundreds of dollars. At our Concerned Black Clergy meetings, Mrs. Hester Johnson and Minister Mmoja Ajabu have monitored the problems for a couple of years through a committee called the Juvenile Justice Committee. Each week an up-date is presented to the Concerned Black Clergy. From what we hear, we are still asking the question: Is there any justice for all? I say, no there is no justice for all unless we make our own justice. Dr. King made us aware that "Injustice anywhere is a threat to justice everywhere." Furthermore, he said,

> *"Justice for black people will not flow into society merely from court decisions nor from fountains of political oratory. Nor will a few token changes quell all the tempestuous yearnings of millions of disadvantaged black people. White America must recognize that justice for black people cannot be achieved without radical changes in the structure of our society."*

I interpret his words to mean that we must do all that we can to make changes in society. This includes making changes in the courts and out of the courts, in the political arena, and especially in the voting booth.

Malcolm X made it crystal clear by addressing issues with these famous words, "By any means necessary." May the means that we use to bring about justice remind us of the sacrifices of those who paved the way for us. As it relates to justice, we can say that everybody seems to have an approach to obtain justice. In *The Autobiography of Malcolm X*, Malcolm wrote,

> *The goal has always been the same, with the approaches to it as different as mine and Dr. Martin Luther King's non-violent marching, that dramatizes the brutality and the evil of the white man against defenseless blacks. And in the racial climate of this country today, it is anybody's guess which of the "extremes" in approach to the black man's problems might personally meet a fatal catastrophe first—"non-violent" Dr. King, or so-called "violent" me. (p. 384)*

Unfortunately, Malcolm and Dr. King were assassinated. I was a senior in high school when Malcolm X, who was born Malcolm Little, was gunned down in New York in 1962. Of course, the whole world was shaken in 1968 by the riveting earthquake, the assassination of our civil rights leader and the 1964 recipient of the Nobel Peace Prize, the Rev. Dr. Martin Luther King, Jr.

When Dr. King was assassinated, I was a senior at Albany State College. I was listening to the car radio when the program was interrupted by this important announcement. I had to park my car at the next stop sign and weep. "Who? Why?" I was devastated. It was as if someone had murdered a very dear and close relative. My heart began to pound and then to ache.

"Oh no!" I sobbed in disbelief. This cannot be. I had marched behind this giant of a man. He had spoken a few words to me in Birmingham. I had often seen him on television. I had read so many newspaper and magazine articles about Dr. King. I had listened to him speak in Albany and in Birmingham. I had walked at the back of the line that he and others led. How could this be? I respected Dr. King so much. "Oh no, he can't be gone."

Then I began to ask God all about it. I was taught in the lesson of an old hymn of the church, "Take everything to God in prayer." These were two of the things that I knew I was going to need, God and prayer. The mere fact that Dr. King was murdered and did not die from natural causes made it so difficult to understand and to accept.

Dr. King was murdered on the balcony of the Lorraine Hotel in Memphis, Tennessee. All attention was focused on Memphis. Who could have done this terrible, terrible act of violence? Who could have snuffed out his life and taken the physical body from the people who loved him? More importantly, who would be so cruel and evil as to deprive the Dr. King's children, Yolanda, Martin, Dexter, and the baby girl, Bernice, of their father? Who would devastate and separate Dr. King from his beautiful and supportive wife, Coretta Scott King?

For years, Mrs. King probably feared and dreaded that Dr. King's life might one day be taken because a woman had stabbed him once in New York. I remembered some of Dr. King's comments on television about that incident. He told the world what the attending doctor had said to him about his wound. I deduced that, had he sneezed during this attack, he would have been pronounced dead at the scene that day.

Today, as I reflect on what Dr. King's loss meant to me as a young person and to others of that time, I hypothesize that American youth find it difficult, or even impossible, to identify civil rights leaders today. Recently I conducted a survey and posed this question, "Who do you say are the three top civil right leaders in this county?" All age groups were included in the survey. The answers to that question proved that my hypothesis was accurate. Many young people did not know any civil rights leaders. A substantial number did not feel that we have any civil rights leaders today. Some only listed the civil rights leaders who are deceased, such as Dr. King. On the other hand, what shocked me the most was that many do not know any civil rights leaders other than Dr. King.

Blessings and Honors Today

The Lord has shown favor on me countless times. I received a beautiful award for being "A Woman of Great Faith," presented by the Greater Atlanta Club of the National Association of Negro Business and Professional Women's Clubs. (NANBPWC) in 2001.

I was awestruck upon learning that I was chosen to receive the Woman of the Year Award in Religion from one of the most productive and prestigious organizations in the country, The Concerned Black Clergy (CBC) in 2002. This organization was founded over twenty years ago by ministers for the purpose of stamping out homelessness. I am a member and serve on the board of directors. I was the chairperson for membership for two years, but I resigned because I needed more time to complete this book, and I was often commuting back and forth to Albany to check on my ailing mother who died in October, 2004.

The Concerned Black Clergy is under the presidential and capable leadership of the Rev. Darrell E. Elligan. Recently, he gave his State of the Community Speech and made some profound statements about the importance of teaching leadership to our youth. When I became a member of the CBC, the President was the Rev. Timothy McDonald who, then, carried a bullhorn around in his car in preparation for marching for any worthy cause. This is one of the reasons that I joined the organization about five years ago. It reminded me of my days marching for freedom and for a better Albany in the Albany Movement.

In the Concerned Black Clergy, we fight for homelessness, the rights of poor people, juvenile justice, voter's education and voters registration, education, prison reform, just to name a few. I am very honored to serve with any group that devotes time to helping people. This is my calling. The songwriter inspired me with words that spoke to me saying, "If I Can Help Somebody Along the Way, Then My Living Shall Not Be In Vain."

About four years ago, I was presented with the Ambassador of Peace Award from the American Clergy Leadership Conference (ACLC) I found out that this award is not about what one has done, rather it is about what one *can do* as it relates to promoting world peace and reconciliation among the three Abrahamic faiths. I have been blessed by "living for the sake of others" and by promoting positive family values with hundreds of interfaith and inter-religious men and women. They are diverse in color, creed, and culture. As I recall, Dr. King spoke of peace, diversity, and living together and holding hands together as blacks and whites, Jews and Gentiles.

It seems that my juvenile beginnings at sixteen were really a springboard to what was to come later. I have come from being a follower to being a leader. My prayer is that my son, Byron, can take my torch and join others of his generation to continue making this world a more peaceful place to live.

In this world of terrorism, suicide bombers, gang banging, drive-by shootings, teen pregnancy, the AIDS crisis, poverty, unemployment, and homelessness, somebody must hear the wake-up call. The clarion call is to help—to help the homeless, to help the hurting, to help the hungry, to help the lost, to help the least and yes, to help those left behind.

We are all here for a purpose. What is your purpose? Why are you here? Why were you born? Time is running out. There is much to be done in so little time. I do believe that we as a people spend too much time criticizing one another, waiting on people to fall and to fail. We spend too much time hating one another. I won't be surprised if someone were to say, who gave her the right to write her opinions? Well, the first Amendment gives me the right. I want the people in my lifetime to come together in unity and in harmony. This book is for posterity. One day I will have to bid you a farewell. But until that time, I am living out my destiny, trying to be the best role model that I can be for my students, my parishioners, my son Byron, and my God-daughters, Keaver, Brandi, and Angela. I want peace in my home, in my church, and wherever I go. Perhaps Rodney King of California never thought that his popular question would outlive him. He asked a question that will live forever: "Can we all get along?" Well, can we?

Prior to writing this book, I distributed a questionnaire. The questions were about who are the top civil rights leaders of today. You would be surprised who were considered to be the civil rights leaders of today. Yes, you'd be surprised to know that many resent or reject the idea that some consider themselves civil rights leaders. It seems that some believe that the printed and the electronic media have ways of printing and promoting whomever they feel are the civil right leaders.

I have a problem with recycling leaders. When one leader dies, others move up and over. However, there never seems to be the older leaders passing the torch or the older leaders grooming younger men and women to continue the fight for justice and equality. There are those in my circle of friends who believe that US Senator Barack Obama of Illinois is moving right on up to the front of the line with much speed. The war is not over. We have won a few battles, but the war continues. We sang the songs of freedom, but the one that resonates in my ears today is "We Shall Overcome, Someday." Either we change the thought that we shall overcome today, or we sing a new song. Maybe our young leaders could give us a song to sing—a song of pride, a song of our rich heritage, a song of unity, a song of destiny, and a song of purpose.

There is a feeling in my spirit—and my God-daughter, Keaver, made me know it when she joined me for the Martin Luther King Day parade in Lawrenceville, Georgia—that the history of civil rights is not understood by all. Keaver is from Iowa. Certainly, in the north and out west, students have not talked about civil rights as much as students in the south, nor have they had the same experiences. I say that race relations should be taught in all schools. Respect for diversity must be taught as requirement.

I believe that all students should read Dr. King's words that Coretta Scott King selected to include in "Civil Rights" p.47:

"The Negro freedom movement would have been historic and worthy even if it had only served the cause of civil rights. But its laurels are greater because it stimulated a boarder social movement that elevated the moral level of the nation. In the struggle against the preponderant evils of the society, decent values were preserved. Moreover, a significant body of young people learned that in opposing the tyrannical forces that were crushing them, they added stature and meaning to their lives. The Negro and white youth whose alliance fought bruising engagements with the status quo inspired each other with a sense of moral mission, and both gave the nation an example of self-sacrifice and dedication."

I am also reminded of a sermon that I preached for the New Year's Eve service at our church as we approached the end of 2005. My sermon was about new wine and old wineskins. If new wine is poured into an old wineskin, the wineskin will burst. New wine must be put into new wineskins. That says to me that our generations to come must be made new before we can pour in new ideas and new directions. There has to be an attitudinal change before new ideas and new directions can make an impact.

Two texts were used to get this message across. First there was the Scripture from Luke 5:38, which reads: "But new wine must be put into new bottles, and both are preserved." If that is the case, then how does one get this new wineskin, this new bottle, or this new container? I found the answer in II Corinthians 5:17. Paul says in the Scripture these words: "Therefore if any man be in Christ, he is a new creature; the old things are passed away; behold, all things are become new."

Although many people who read this book may not read the Holy Bible, I must write the truth. You see, the truth will set us free. One has to become a new creature, a new creation, in order for the new wine to last, not be destroyed, or become wasted. When the newness comes and the old passes away, then, and only then, can we receive into ourselves, as vessels, the new wine that has been destined for our lives. New wine—new ideas, new dreams, new direction—placed in new wineskins, new vessels, will not perish. It will not ruin, but it will last from generation to generation. Our youth must become new vessels, become more spiritual, and seek God as I and as many of their parents did at an early age.

Many still debate the idea of whether God calls female pastors. I never waste time debating about whom God has called. I do not debate what God has called me to do. There is too much work to be done. As a matter of fact, God, not only called me to be a pastor, but God also prepared me to be a pastor. Then God allowed me to make a strong impact in the church in which I was assigned. The church has flourished and that was and is, all, a part of God's plan.

Just as I know that God called me to teach for a quarter century, God called me to pastor the churches that I have pastored. Almighty God has called me to teach, to preach, and to reach the masses. As I serve as a community leader, I continue to crusade against the evils that oppress God's people. We, who marched and protested, shouted down the walls of racism and discrimination. However, we must continue to stay on the wall. Why? Because racism and discrimination continue. We were on a mission then, and we are on a mission now.

As pastor, human rights activist, teacher, wife, and parent, I continue to crusade against anything that oppresses God's people, especially the downtrodden and God's people of color. No matter if I am given credit or not, I still fight for all people against injustices in the world. My reward comes from my Maker, my Creator, my Sustainer, the Author and Finisher of my faith, my Lord and Savior, the One who has brought me through the valley and up the rocky mountains of life. Still, I am "no ways tired." My God has brought me through dangers seen and unseen. My God has brought me full circle from the back of the line to lead others with the same dignity, with the same pride, and with the same courage, with which I followed. Thanks be to God for the things that He has done in my life starting "from the back of the line."

Rev. Dr. Gloria Ward Wright praying and preparing for the Dr. Martin Luther King, Jr., Day parade and rally at the courtyard square in Lawrenceville, GA.

In Lawrenceville Dr. Wright gets to converse with the leaders of Gwinnett County where her church is located. She shakes hands with Georgia's State Senator Curt Thompson at the King Day march. (L-R in the background) Mayor Jerry Oberholtzer of Snellville and Mayor Bobby Sikes of Lawrenceville, Georgia.

(L-R) Dr. Gloria W. Wright talks with Pastor Tony Brock of Hope and Life Fellowship Church of Snellville about her book. Pastor Brock brought his two sons to the King Day Rally.

(L-R) Mrs. Robbie Moore, Rev. Dr. Gloria Ward Wright, Mrs. Yoshiko Toyomura, and Ms. Keaver Brenai at the King Day Rally at Lawrenceville's old courthouse.

(L-R) Rev. Dr. Gloria Ward Wright and civil rights leader, Rev. C.T. Vivian are seated at a meeting in Atlanta as he writes a quotation for her book.
(Photo) Dr. Ann Smith—Gamaliel Foundation—Chicago

Dr. Gloria Ward Wright participated on a panel as one of the speakers at a Youth Conference on Education and Service, Washington D.C.

(L-R) Rev. Dr. Merchuria Chase Williams, a friend of many years and the President of the Georgia Association of Educators standing with Dr. Wright at a Concerned Black Clergy Meeting.

Rev. Dr. Wright praying in Jerusalem at the Western Wall for the unity of the three Abrahamic faiths, the Jews, the Muslims, and the Christians.

A current photograph of Kay Smith Pedrotti and her husband, Robert "Bob" Pedrotti. —Courtesy of Excalibur, Atlanta

Mrs. Janice S. Andrews, general manager of the Capitol City Bank Building and wife of President George Andrews, of the Capitol City Bank Building pins Dr. Wright's corsage as she is saluted a "Woman of Faith," an honor bestowed on Dr. Wright by the Greater Atlanta Club of the NANBPWC, the National Association of Negro Business and Professional Women's Club.

A very dear and loyal friend, Mrs. Yoshiko Toyomura, a former missionary from Japan, teaches love by example. She and her husband, Tommy, enjoy giving love and flowers to others.

Viewing God's universe a top Mt. Nebo (left to right) Archbishop Moses de la Rosa, Bishop Margie de la Rosa, and Rev. Dr. Gloria Ward Wright.

The dedicated leadership team at Simmons Chapel A.M.E. Zion Church in Lawrenceville, Georgia. (L-R) Mrs. Dianne Evans, deaconess, Rev. Emmanuel T. Solo, associate minister, Rev. Dr. Gloria Ward Wright, pastor, and Mrs. Maude Jones-Solo, deaconess.

Rev. Dr. Gloria Ward Wright, in the pulpit, preaching the Word of God on Communion Sunday. (Photo) Courtesy of Your Precious Moment.

Rev. Dr Gloria Ward. Wright stands alone in the sanctuary of Simmons Chapel African Methodist Episcopal Zion Church, the "Little Church Where Miracles Happen."

(L-R—top row) Ministerial friends: Rev. Margrite M. Roberts, Rev. Dr. Margaret Richardson, and Rev. Dr. Jeannette T. Holt. (Seated) Dr. Gloria Ward Wright. Among Dr. Wright's many devoted friends and prayer partners are Mrs. Sherma Owens, Mrs. Dianne Evans, and Ms. Amy Holland who share in Dr. Wright's ministry. (Not pictured in this photograph)

(L-R) The late Mrs. Eldonia ("Mama Julie ") Washington seen in this picture with Rev. Dr. Gloria Ward Wright at church. Mrs. Washington called Gloria, "My other daughter." Dr. Wright loved all people, but seniors and youth stole her heart.

(L-R) Atlanta's Mayor Shirley Franklin takes time to take a photograph with Dr. Wright at the Mayor's Annual Senior Citizen's Ball.

Rev. Timothy McDonald, Past President of the Concerned Black Clergy presents Dr. Wright with an award at a banquet for outstanding contributions in the area of religion. Rev. John Bartley and Ms. Yolanda Reynolds share the moment.

Mr. Byron Ward Wright teaches the children in children's church at Simmons Chapel AME Zion Church. Directly behind Byron are Ms. Keaver Brenai and Ms. R. Pamela Adams.

Initially there were only three members when Dr. Gloria Ward Wright was assigned as pastor at Simmons Chapel A.M.E. Zion Church in Lawrenceville. In this photograph are some of the most faithful and dedicated members who have joined her in ministry.

EPILOGUE

I leave you a responsibility to our young people: Our children must never lose their zeal for building a better world. They must not be discouraged from aspiring to greatness. Nor must they forget that the masses of our people are still underprivileged, ill-housed, impoverished, and victimized by discrimination.

The Freedom Gates are half ajar. We must pry them fully open.

I leave you—my generation, today's youth, and future generations—with inspiration from two great "Front of the Line" leaders, Mary McLeod Bethune and Desmond Tutu.

My Last Will and Testament

If I have a legacy to leave my people, it is my philosophy of living and serving. Here, then, is My Legacy . . .

- I leave you love.

    Love builds. It is positive and helpful.

- I leave you hope.

    Yesterday, our ancestors endured the degradation of slavery, yet they retained their dignity.

- I leave you the challenge of developing confidence in one another.

    This kind of confidence will aid the economic rise of the race by bringing together the pennies and dollars of our people and ploughing them into useful channels.

- I leave you thirst for education.

    Knowledge is the prime need of the hour.

- I leave you a respect for the uses of power.

    Power, intelligently directed, can lead to more freedom.

- I leave you faith.

  Faith in God is the greatest power, but great, too, is faith in oneself.

- I leave you racial dignity.

  I want Negroes to maintain their human dignity at all costs.

- I leave you a desire to live harmoniously with your fellow man.
- I leave you, finally, a responsibility to our young people.

  The world around us really belongs to youth; for youth will take over its future management.

  —Mary McLeod Bethune

"We can be truly free, ultimately, only together . . . black and white, rich and poor, Christian, Muslim, Hindu, Buddhist, and Jew . . . God's dream wants us to be brothers and sisters, wants us to be family."

  —Archbishop Desmond Tutu
  Nobel Laureate

APPENDIX

Quotable Quotes from Notables on Civil Rights

"The ultimate measure of a man is not where he stands in moments of comfort and convenience, but where he stands at times of challenge and controversy."
—Rev. Martin Luther King, Jr.

Many memorable quotations came out of the civil rights movement, perhaps none better expressed than Dr. King's statement above. But what is said about the movement today? Are we keeping the flame alive with our words? Are we teaching the next generation?

While writing this book, it occurred to me that I really needed to know how others feel about civil rights. Would they see civil rights as I do? What do adults feel? What do the youth of today feel? So I devised a simple survey to poll a sample of people about their opinions on civil rights, then and now. Those who responded to my survey included a former and present superintendent of the Atlanta Public schools, the mayor of Atlanta, the former assistant superintendent of Fulton County Schools, the immediate past president of the Concerned Black Clergy, the southern regional director of Rainbow PUSH, a clinical psychologist, some of the top civil rights leaders of our times, and many church leaders.

I also surveyed people from my past who were active in the movement: my seventh grade homeroom teacher, one of the original Freedom Singers, her brother, a freedom fighter and childhood friend. I polled a friend who became a North Carolina state senator, as well as many church members, friends, and a host of community leaders, teachers, and church officials. Most importantly, many of my former students participated in the survey.

I asked all of them nine questions to learn their views about the need to give young people today positive reminders of the civil rights struggle. I asked older people if they had marched with Dr. King or participated in other demonstrations. I asked youth if they had relatives who had participated, and I asked youth, "Would you go to jail in order to protect your civil rights?"

I received many wonderful responses. Some are listed below. Others, which endorse this book, are listed on the inside back pages and on the back cover. I included many of these notable quotations here in the hope that they will inspire young people and enlighten them about the critical importance of understanding our history:

"If we do not tell our history, then at best it will be misinterpreted, at worst, the history will be lost."

—Minister Mmoja Ajabu,
Concerned Black Clergy

*   *   *

"The difficulties and problems that African-Americans of all ages suffered for the last five generations was the outgrowth of attitudes and myths held toward people of color. Youth of all races need to read how we overcame those imposed difficulties so they can properly appreciate their new freedoms."

—Dr. C. T. Vivian,
Civil Rights Leader, Atlanta

*   *   *

"Youth need to be involved in civil rights today more than ever before."

—Bishop Murjan A. Rasheed,
Holy Spirit of Promise Outreach Ministries,
Inc. Atlanta

*   *   *

"We must see that our schools provide to all students a true history of this nation. It is important that each subject integrates the history of our people in all classes. Schools are obligated to adapt and adjust the learning environment so as to assume that all students learn. ALL STUDENTS CAN LEARN."

—Dr. J. Jerome Harris,
Former Superintendent,
Atlanta Public Schools

*   *   *

"History is a bright star shining from behind us, from the path we have come that illuminates and punctuates the path that is before us. History is us! We are history! God is good."

—Dr. Henry Braddock,
Clinical psychologist, Atlanta

*   *   *

"As we shape our children's legacy, we must understand that the struggles for equality and the value of education to a free society are permanently linked."
—Beverly L. Hall, Ed. D.,
Superintendent, Atlanta Public Schools

*   *   *

"Children of today live in a totally different world than we did in the forties, the fifties, and the sixties. Their thought patterns are influenced by the media and their peers. This is because children are coming from so many broken homes without a two-parent image as we had. Unless we start to rebuild the nation, there can be no peace on earth as Jesus prayed, "Thy kingdom come, Thy will be done.""
—Apostle W. R. Malcolm,
Triumph the Church and
Kingdom of God in Christ, Atlanta

*   *   *

"In 1959 and 1960 in Wilmington, North Carolina, I participated in the original boycotts against Woolworth Stores and Rose's Five and Dime Store. This was for black employment, and later we were involved in the lunch counter sit-ins at the same location."
—Rev. Robert Kilgore, associate minister,
Hillside Chapel and Truth Center, Atlanta

*   *   *

"Who is Martin Luther King, Jr.? Who is Ralph David Abernathy? Who is Andrew Young? Who is Gloria Ward Wright? And what are they to me? What have they done for me . . . ever? Since I raise the question, do you wonder if I am from another country or a newborn baby? Am I blind, mute, deaf, illiterate, AND out of touch? Or am I from the Midwest where African-American studies were not offered as a class elective, or possibly am I from a multi-cultural family that didn't focus on African-American history? Well, the question still stands, 'Who am I and who are they?' My generation wants and needs to know . . ."

—Keaver Brenai, my Godchild,
born in the 1960s

*   *   *

"The theme for Martin Luther King, Jr. Week, 2005, is: 'Let us turn to each other and not on each other to stop violence.' This I believe!"

—The Reverend James Orange,
Civil Rights Activist /
Atlanta Concerned Black Clergy

*   *   *

"We as adult leaders must find a way to educate our young people to what the civil rights movement is all about. They really don't know. By way of the schools, we can help them to understand what it was. On top of that, we must educate the teachers, for many of the younger teachers do not know what took place during the civil rights movement. The school is best where the teaching can be done. From there we can establish leadership. If we can educate others, then we will see ourselves as individual leaders."

—Dr. Barbara L. King, Pastor
Hillside Truth Center, Atlanta

*   *   *

"Youth today should be learning their culture and their heritage which is their history. Without their history, there is no hope for the future. Those who forget their past or those who don't know their past cannot know their future destiny, for they know not from which they have come."

—Elder William "Bill" Harris,
Civil Rights Activist and
SCLC Freedom Singer

*   *   *

"The world into which I was born is not the world in which I live because of the personal sacrifice of Dr. Martin Luther King, Jr."

—Mayor Shirley Franklin, Atlanta

*   *   *

"The sixties shaped a social movement in the U.S. with civil rights and equality of opportunity, regardless of age, sex, color, or creed for every citizen atop its agenda. It compelled the black youth of the day to step out on faith and, in the spirit of Frederick Douglass, 'agitate' through coordinated and collective action to set in motion and bring about unprecedented changes in the U.S.

"The nineties ushered in an era of 'political correctness' where diversity became the buzz word around the country. Unlike their parents' generation, the youth of the nineties seemed to lack the temerity and vision that so characterized their parents' generation. This aura spilled over into the new millennium and still holds true today. Is this merely a lack of interest amongst the youth? Maybe the civil rights gains have insulated them from the *de facto* and the *de jure* segregation and bigotry of the sixties? Or maybe their elders have not passed along the way things used to be for blacks in the U.S.

"The new millennium youth have not had to wait in line. They have no appreciation of 'separate but equal' facilities. Since their parents did not and do not impress upon them the value sets that characterized their upbringing, does their apathy genuinely surprise anyone? Although they have not demonstrated the attitude and the fortitude of their parents, they can muster and put forth a coordinated and sustained effort to keep at bay the sentiments that led to policies and attitudes that once confirmed a marginal existence for black America. These same youth must look to themselves and not to an outside culture or community to define what the future holds for them. If not, they will succumb to the role of voluntary victim and find themselves once again in the back of the line."

—Felix Brown, 40, former student;
Network engineer, Atlanta

*   *   *

"On the subject of civil rights and youth, a white female of the Concerned Black Clergy writes, 'There is no greater hope for freedom and social justice than our youth. They *must* be taught the urgent history of dissent in order to protect our civil and human rights.'"

—Anita Beasley, advocate for the homeless and
member of Concerned Black Clergy

*   *   *

"Civil rights today are under severe attack from every level of government. The 'Haves' are opposing the 'Have-nots.' Education is under attack; privacy is under assault; voting rights are being denied; and the rights of the elderly are being curtailed. It is time to wake up."

—Rev. Timothy McDonald, III,
Immediate past president of
Concerned Black Clergy and pastor of
First Iconium Baptist Church, Atlanta

*   *   *

"My experience with the civil rights movement also started when I was a teenager of fifteen in Greenwood, S.C., where I started the first youth NAACP chapter. The youth charter was signed and organized in our home because other organizations, i.e., churches, American Legion, were afraid for us to meet and black churches didn't want to get involved."

—Dr. Rhunett R. Lindsey,
Concerned Black Clergy

*   *   *

"During my high school days, I participated in the civil rights movement and voter registration. I also participated as a member of the SNCC, walking through neighborhoods and encouraging others to register to vote. During this period there was total segregation. Blacks were not allowed in certain places or many places. The goal was to encourage people to exercise their rights. After school we met with Charles Sherrod to canvas the neighborhoods. We were quite fearful because the police watched our every move. We conquered that fear. Then we moved to outside counties (Lee, Terrell, Worth, Baker, and Calhoun Counties). We organized sit-ins at restaurant counters, etc. We were terrorized, but we struggled on. The movement became stronger in Dougherty and other surrounding counties. Our faith strengthened as we went to jail by the thousands. We marched downtown.

"Then one night I received a call. I was asked to go sing from town-to-town with the movement. My mother was reluctant, but my sisters and friends encouraged her to allow me to go. God had to bless the plan because we conquered so much. We prayed, we sang, we marched from Selma, Alabama, to Mississippi, to Birmingham, Alabama. We fought for justice and we still have a long ways to go. Through it all, with God's help, 'We Shall Overcome.'"

—Emory L. Harris,
Albany Movement singer

*   *   *

"I grew up in a loving community in south Georgia where the familiar phrase, 'It takes a village to raise a child' was taken seriously. Everyone shared in the responsibility of raising the children. Discipline and guidance of all children in the community was number one among all the adults. Also in that community, bartering and sharing were a common practice, from food and clothes to transportation.

"The civil rights movement did a wonderful job of securing our freedom, but in so doing, we forgot to teach the responsibility that goes along with freedom. My prayer is that the movement will recognize this serious omission and begin to make the necessary corrections. For example, black males have two strikes against them when they come into this world, so unless they are educated (which takes a lot of patience on our part as parents) they will be lost, and eventually become a statistical casualty."

—Eugene Dryer, Ph.D.,
Former southern regional director of the
National Education Association

*   *   *

"I became involved in the civil rights movement during the summer of 1961 in Albany, Georgia, after completing one year of college at Florida A&M University in Tallahassee, Florida. My involvement in the Albany Movement was that of a song leader and a field secretary for the Student Nonviolent Coordinating Committee (SNCC). I had the opportunity to sing songs at the mass meetings; these songs included short meter hymns, congregational singing, spirituals, and gospel. I also participated in marches, prayer vigils, and picket lines. I was jailed three times and spend a total of fourteen days in the city and county jails of Albany and Leesburg, Georgia.

"As a field secretary of SNCC, I would canvass the city to get people registered to vote and encourage them to go back to the polls and vote on election day. We would also encourage them to come to the mass meetings to become actively involved in the struggle that was going on in their city.

"During the Albany Movement, the original freedom singers were organized by the late Cordell Reagon. This group, including Charles Neblett and Bernice Johnson Reagon, was formed to raise funds for SNCC to continue fighting injustices throughout the South. The group traveled 50,000 miles, covered forty-eight states in nine months, and told the stories of the movement through songs."

—Miss Rutha Mae Harris,
Original freedom singer

*   *   *

"Of course, with the death/assassination of Dr. King, it almost became 'the Violent Death of Nonviolence!' Through God's grace, however, it brought about a new awakening in the human rights struggle that maintains hope for a bloodless revolution in our lifetime!"

—Tony R. Graves (AKA) Babatunde Harith
O'mawali, Conscious Wear, Inc.

*   *   *

"Being a child of a history teacher, I have learned that the most important information is found in the past through connection with the present. I am a child of the integration era which caused disillusionment of my generation. A false sense of stability invades the black community's psyche. We need more books, information, and insight into the civil rights struggle, especially from African-American women."

—Aaron Naeem Robinson,
Son a history instructor
(In Memory of Mrs. Juanita Turner)

*   *   *

"Over the past forty years, blood, sweat, and tears have been shed, and sometimes lives were lost in the just cause of equal and civil rights of black Americans. We have come a long way from the days of passing by Shoney's and Holiday Inns, to pulling into these places for a nice meal and a good night's rest. We must yet have an agenda for advancement and equal access—the Dreamer's dream is not yet realized."

—Rev. Don C. Phillips, Jr.,
Presiding elder, Atlanta-Summerville
District, Georgia Conference,
The African Methodist Episcopal Zion Church

*   *   *

"In a time when teenagers need to be aware of new forms of oppression and denial, some literature is critical in direct terms. Most teenagers have no real knowledge of the manifestations of forces more wicked and more destructive that are circulating, and this violence is systemic. Knowledge from experience is real and will open young eyes to reality."

—Dr. Ndugu G. B. T'Ofori-atta,
Faith A.M.E. Zion Church,
The Interdenominational Theological
Seminary (ITC) Atlanta

*   *   *

"Being an active participant in the movement that took place in downtown Atlanta, I witnessed the horrific acts that our people had to endure and felt it an honor to be drenched by hoses and battered by rocks. The youth of today must be reminded of the price that was paid in order for them to experience and appreciate the freedom that they have. They must possess it with pride, never losing sight of the cause. We have come a long way, but still have a long way to go before we can claim freedom. Hopefully, many will read this book and will pick up the mantle and continue to move forward."

—Dr. Shirley M. Phillips,
Former assistant superintendent,
Fulton County Board of Education

*   *   *

"I believe African-Americans have become too comfortable with our status in today's society. Black history and the civil rights movement have been forgotten, and the youth today really have no idea of the sacrifice of life, time, freedom, blood, sweat, and tears of our ancestors."

—Alisha Danielle Ward, 23,
Albany State University graduate

*   *   *

"I will be nice to all people because it doesn't matter what color you are."

—Conner Brock, 11,
Hope and Life Fellowship, Snellville, GA

*   *   *

"Young people need to know how we got over, how we had many obstacles to overcome. They need to know about legal segregation. They need to know about colored water, colored toilets, and all of the problems that we faced. They need to know that many of the problems still exists. Teach them and they will learn."

—Henry E. Brown,
Retired educator,
Omega Psi Phi Fraternity, Decatur, GA

*   *   *

"In today's world teens don't feel like civil rights are that important, simply because they feel that the 'fight' is over. My family has been involved in civil rights by way of my great aunt, Rosa Parks. I know first hand that in order to keep this so-called 'peace,' we must continue on our way to equality and everlasting freedom. Without us, we would be doomed."

—Whitney Carnes, 17,
Gwinnett Technical School

*   *   *

"I believe my Aunt Rosa Parks' legacy will live on through us. She inspires us to stand up against in justices in our everyday lives."

—Susan McCauley-Brown,
Rosa Parks' niece,
Lawrenceville, GA

*   *   *

"I think that it is still great that we appreciate the works of Dr. Martin Luther King, Jr."

—Thomas Keys, 18 years old

*   *   *

"I went to jail a couple of times. After I was arrested, it occurred to me that I was the reigning Miss Debutante. I thought to myself, 'How will this look for me, a queen, to be locked up in jail?'"

—Barbara R. Willis,
1962 graduate, Monroe High School, and
former employee of Albany State College

THE CIVIL RIGHTS ACT OF 1964

O ne of the most important accomplishments of the civil rights era was the Civil Rights Act of 1964. Passage of this law validated much of what we had marched, demonstrated, sang, and been jailed for in the preceding years. I include some background and a summary of this law in the hope that readers—young and old—will review and appreciate its significance in improving the lives of all people.

When President John F. Kennedy was assassinated in November 1963, most civil rights leaders were distraught because Kennedy was the first president since Harry Truman to champion equal rights for black Americans. Many leaders worried about whether JFK's Southern successor, Lyndon Baines Johnson, would continue Kennedy's call for civil rights. But five days after the assassination, the newly sworn in President Johnson addressed the Congress and the nation for the first time and called for passage of the civil rights bill as a monument to Kennedy.

Johnson declared, "Let us continue," and promised that "the ideas and the ideals which [Kennedy] so nobly represented must and will be translated into effective action." Johnson used his considerable talents as a legislative arm-twister, as well as the prestige of the Presidency, to support the bill. The House of Representatives passed the measure by a 290-130 vote in February 1964, but the real battle would be in the Senate, whose rules had allowed Southerners to mount filibusters that had effectively killed nearly all civil rights legislation in the past. But Johnson pulled every string he knew, and civil rights leaders mounted a powerful lobbying campaign, including flooding the Capitol with religious leaders of all faiths and of all colors. In early June, the Senate passed the most important piece of civil rights legislation in the nation's history with 73 Senators in favor and 27 against. President Johnson signed it into law on July 2, 1964. There were several parts to it called "Titles" summarized below:

Title One concerned voting: Literacy tests had been given in order to register to vote in many states. This title stated that blacks and whites had to be given the same test. (The practice was later banned by the federal Voting Rights Act of 1965.)

Title Two banned discrimination in such places as hotels, motels, restaurants, and theaters. This brought an end to Jim Crow customs.

Title Three opened up public accommodations: Black Americans had to be treated the same as whites in all public parks, swimming pools, beaches, and stadiums.

Title Four concerned public schools: All public schools had to be desegregated by the order of the courts to obey their rulings.

Title Five validated the Civil Rights Commission. If someone felt that his or her civil rights were violated, the commission acted as a watchdog to make sure that rights were not being violated.

Title Six banned federal aid to any state and locality that discriminated in its programs.

Title Seven prohibited discrimination in businesses and unions. Today this applies when there are twenty-five or more workers.

Title Eight allowed government to keep records of how many blacks can and do vote. There can be quick action on those in the South who were not allowed to vote.

Title Nine allowed the federal courts to order lower courts to rule quickly rather than stall for time (sending cases back and forth), as federal judges in the South had often delayed decisions in civil rights cases. This title encompassed the saying, "Justice delayed is Justice denied."

Title Ten concerned the Community Relations Service whose job was to try to settle racial problems at the local level. The idea was to prevent small problems from growing into big problems.

Title Eleven addressed other rights; for example, this title promised a jury trial to those who were punished by judges for not obeying the law; to not upset state laws that gave the same rights that the law promised; and if a title was found not to be allowed by the Constitution, then only that title would end.

SUGGESTED READING

Branch, Taylor. *Parting the Waters: America in the King Years, 1954-1963*. New York: Simon and Schuster, 1988.

Carson, Clayborne. "SNCC and the Albany Movement," *Journal of Southwest Georgia History* 2, 1984: 15-25.

Chalfen, Michael. "Rev. Samuel B. Wells and Black Protest in Albany, 1945-1965," *Journal of Southwest Georgia History* 9, 1994: 37-64.

Da Silva, Benjamin, et al. *The Afro-American in United States History*. New York: Globe Book Company, 2d edition, 1972.

Hughes, Langston, Milton Meltzer, and C. Eric Lincoln. *African-American History*. New York: Scholastic, Inc., 1990.

Jenkins, Mary Royal. *Open Dem Cells: A Pictorial History of the Albany Movement,* Columbus, Georgia: Brentwood Academic Press, 2000.

Katz, William Loren, and Warren J. Halliburton, *A History of Black Americans*. New York: Harcourt Brace Jovanovich, Inc., 1973.

King, Coretta Scott (editor). *The Words of Martin Luther King, Jr.* New York: Newmarket Press, 2001.

Lewis, John and Michael D'Orso. *Walking with the Wind: A Memoir of the Movement.* New York: Simon and Schuster, 1998.

Lyon, Danny. *Memories of the Southern Civil Rights Movement*. Chapel Hill: University of North Carolina Press, 1992.

McKissack, Patricia and Fredrick. *The Civil Rights Movement From 1865 to the Present,* 2nd Edition. Chicago: Children's Press, 1991.

Parks, Rosa, with Gregory J. Reed. *Quiet Strength: The Faith, the Hope, and the Heart of a Woman Who Changed a Nation.* Grand Rapids, Michigan: Zondervan Publishing House, 1994.

Rochelle, Belinda. *Witnesses To Freedom: Young People Who Fought For Civil Rights.* New York: Puffin Books, 1997.

Steven G. N. *Beyond Atlanta: The Struggle for Racial Equality in Georgia, 1940-1980.* Athens: University of Georgia Press, 2001.

Walls, Bishop William J. *The African Methodist Episcopal Zion Church: The Reality of the Black Church.* Charlotte, North Carolina: 1974.

Williams, Juan. *Eyes on the Prize: America's Civil Rights Years, 1954-1965* New York: Penguin, 1988.

Young, Andrew. *An Easy Burden: The Civil Rights Movement and the Transformation of America.* New York: HarperCollins, 1996.

Young, Andrew. *A Way Out Of No Way.* Nashville: Thomas Nelson Publishers, 1994. www.georgiaencyclopedia.org—A project of the Georgia Humanities Council

STATEMENTS OF ENDORSEMENT:
FROM THE BACK OF THE LINE

"A book of this nature is sorely needed to embrace the current civil right movements and activities, and to inspire and inform the youth of our nation and the world."
—Rev. Israel Taylor, retired school counselor and associate minister, Beulah Baptist Church

*   *   *

"Being in the eye of the storm not only gives Dr. Wright the right to write but also the obligation of revelation."*—Mrs. Vivian Brown, retired educator, WH&OM Society*

*   *   *

"This is a positive reminder of the civil rights struggle for our young people. There is no book out there, that I know of, that has any sense of deep struggle that youth in Albany and surrounding counties in southwest Georgia had to go through."
—Rev. Charles Sherrod, civil right leader, Albany Movement

*   *   *

"I think this book is a great idea!" *Brittney Long, 18, Chapel Hills High School*

*   *   *

"Young people helped to energize the civil rights movement in the 1960s. Too many of our young people today seem disconnected from our struggle. One reason for this inactivity may center around a sense of powerlessness. I believe this book detailing your involvement will motivate other young people to get involved. Your valuable contributions as a youth of sixteen will be inspirational."
—Joe Beasley, southern regional director of PUSH, Concerned Black Clergy

*   *   *

"I really appreciate Dr. Wright's determination to write *From the Back of the Line*. As a witness of some pages of U.S. history, she tells her experiences to the next generation and to future generations."—*Yoshiko Toyomura, Japanese friend*

*   *   *

"We need to know the stories of those who were there, young and old."
—*Akbar Imhotep, story teller, Atlanta*

*   *   *

"This book is overdue in its need not only to teach teens, but uninvolved adults. It is also necessary for those of us who were active in the movement, such as myself. I am sure the book will remind us, 'lest we forget.' Just as the Holocaust is a major event in the lives of the Jewish people, the civil rights movement should be a daily reminder that there are many strategists out there trying to move us 'to the back of the line.' Thank you, Dr. Wright, for being led by the still small voice of God to keep us mindful of 'we have come' and we can't go back. After all, we are the righteous of God!"
—*Betty Stephens, school social worker, co-director, Children Atlanta, Summerville District, Georgia District, A.M.E. Zion Church*

*   *   *

"Often youth view our living historians who lived through the movement as holding to a time that no longer exists. Dr. Wright's work will allow them to see vicariously how key youth were in the movement and how important it is for the youth to be vigilant in keeping and expanding the rights of all people, especially minorities and the poor."
—*Merchuria Chase Williams, Ph.D., President of the Georgia Association of Educators*

*   *   *

"Youth must be educated about the struggles of yesterday. They should be made aware of the strides that were made in the 1960s. *From the Back of the Line* will help the youth to see a better today and a better tomorrow."
—*Donzella James, Georgia State Senator (1993-2003)*

*   *   *

"The youth need to be educated about our civil rights. Dr. Wright's book, *From the Back of the Line* is a necessity for our youth of today."
—*Rev. Ethel Newton, Prison Ministries, Atlanta, Georgia*

* * *

"I believe that this type book will be an inspiration to our youth, as well as the older generation, so that we will not forget where we came from, how we got here, and how far we still have to go as African-Americans in these United States."
—*Rev. Margrite M. Roberts, graduate student, Dallas Theological Seminary*

* * *

"This book is a very important resource to help youth and adults to fully understand our struggles during the 1960s, especially written from a youth's perspective."
—*Dr. Rhunett R. Lindsey, educator, Atlanta Public Schools*

* * *

"This book is needed. The young people I teach, PK-5, don't know their history."
—*Arietha Lockhart, musician and educator, Dekalb County School System*

* * *

"I feel that **From the Back of the Line** is an excellent idea. It tells the story of a courageous woman and her fight for civil rights. I strongly believe that the youth of today should be more involved in their community and try and help the homeless and the less fortunate in any way they can."—*Charles Butler, 15, Gospel recording artist, Georgia*

* * *

"**From the Back of the Line** should be an inspiration to many young people like me, to let them know that they too can follow the dream and follow in the footsteps of Dr. Martin Luther King, Jr."—*Taylor Butler, 13, Gospel recording artist, Georgia*

* * *

"I commend Rev. Wright for taking the time to share her experience as a young person. It is through courageous people like her who provide a safety net for the young people of today. If today's youth have no awareness of our history, they will be unable to recognize the impending dangers confronting them. They would therefore be doomed to suffer the potential dangers and oppressions of the past."
—*Rev. Dr. Arthur L. Hilson, past president,*
American Baptist Churches of Vermont and New Hampshire

* * *

"To see and be beyond 'the dream' is to act upon each day, seeing hope beyond possibilities . . . We support your work."

—*Fred "V-Man" Watson, founder,*
Victory Over Violence International Campaign USA-Japan

*   *   *

"It is important that our children learn and understand the sacrifices made to ensure the civil liberties enjoyed by African-Americans today. Through no fault of their own, many of them are unaware of the struggles and they take things for granted. Hopefully, this book will be the beginning of teaching them about the struggles and the rich history and accomplishments of African-Americans in this country."

—*Emmett D. Johnson, member, Atlanta Board of Education*

*   *   *

"I think that talking about the Civil Rights Movement from a teenager's perspective is truly unique."—*Rev. John Bartley, St. John Baptist Church, Atlanta, Ga.*

"To Gloria Ward Wright: Thanks for being an important part of the Albany civil rights movement. You made a brighter day for young African-Americans."

—*Mrs. Mary F. Jenkins, retired Georgia teacher*

*   *   *

"This book may be used to relate to all ages that civil rights movements are a lifetime struggle. It's not something you achieve in two years, four years, or even twenty years, but it's a continuous struggle. You may accomplish some things, but lose something else. So it's a continuous struggle. With God all things are possible. Congratulations to you for such an endeavor."—*Ina Brothers, former teacher and administrator*

*   *   *

"From the Back of the Line is an asset for our youth of today."

—*Bishop Joseph Johnson, retired Bishop,*
African Methodist Episcopal Zion Church, South Carolina

*   *   *

"There is no question that the past has its influences upon the present and future. Thus, it is of the utmost importance that our youth are aware of and understand those persuasive historical influences. The author of this book seeks to present and illuminate significant aspects of African-American experiences in this country, emphasizing the special relevance to the development of America. Special attention is focused upon the unusual problems and frustrations confronted by African-Americans as they struggled to shape their own identity.

"The author, Gloria Ward Wright, was one of my bright, talented, and energetic students during the 1960s. Having been a significant, direct participant in the civil rights movement of that era, she is seeking to heighten the awareness and understanding of our youth relative to the presence, struggle, and accomplishments of African-American in the United States. It is the author's aim to help our youth find the intellectual tools to deal with the remaining problems, as we continue to move toward the ideal of brotherhood. This informative and illuminating book is a valuable resource for guidance and direction relative to some critical concerns that face us today."

—*Charles P. Mobley, Associate Professor Emeritus, Albany State University*

* * *

"I have known Rev. Dr. Gloria Wright for over twenty-five years. Therefore, I know the story of her participation in the Albany, Georgia, civil rights movement when she was a high school student. I admire Dr. Wright for the maturity, commitment, and courage she showed at such a young age. The youth of today, particularly in the South, take their freedom and privileges for granted. They know about Dr. Martin Luther King. Jr., but they don't know about the young foot soldiers like Dr. Wright who were very much a part of the movement and contributed greatly to the freedoms and opportunities young people enjoy today. Dr. Wright's story should be required reading for teenagers. I believe that they will be surprised, inspired, and motivated after reading her story. The story of Kay Smith's full circle conversion from her past is worthy of an appearance on "Oprah" by Gloria and Kay. Hopefully, *From the Back of the Line* will be selected by Oprah for her book club."—*Isaiah Washington, retired federal manager, East Point, Georgia*

* * *

"*From the Back of the Line* should be placed in the library of every African Methodist Episcopal (A.M.E.) Zion church."

—*Walt Bellamy, Basketball Hall of Famer,*
Public Affairs Consultant, College Park, Georgia

* * *

"I believe teenagers should learn how the desegregation efforts were a part of a movement which involved thousands of people. I believe they need to know that it was not one minister (like Martin King, Ralph Abernathy, or Andrew Young), nor was it one woman like Rosa Parks. It was thousands who refused to bow any longer at the altar of segregation!"

—*Rev. Dr. Jeremiah A. Wright, Jr., Pastor,*
Trinity United Church of Christ, Chicago, Illinois

*   *   *

"*From the Back of the Line* is vitally important because many of our young people are not aware of the civil rights struggle that brought about so many of the privileges that they enjoy today. This book is a must for posterity."

—*Bishop Clarence Carr, Prelate, South Atlantic Episcopal District,*
African Methodist Episcopal Zion Church

*   *   *

"*From the Back of the Line* gives a unique perspective of the civil rights movement from one of its unheralded participants. Through the eyes of a child, Dr. Wright gives insight that is both revealing and refreshing."

—*Pastor Daniel Simmons, pastor of my family's home church,*
the new Mt. Zion Baptist Church, Albany, Georgia

*   *   *

"*From the Back of the Line* embodies the truth of a time past, and at the same time links to the present and makes the critical connection of the ages, setting the stage for a time yet to come. Through the eyes of Dr. Wright, the legacy of hope lives on for many who will gain a deeper appreciation for the perseverance of one who God allowed to experience the long range view of that which was to come 'from the back of the line.' As written in Matthew 19:30: 'But many who are first will be last, and many who are last will be first.'"

—*Wanda F. Vinson, telecommunications consultant, Mitchellville, MD*

*   *   *

"The true poet is said to transcend logic into a kind of divine reasoning, wherein the whole of existence is displayed in colossal cosmic symmetry; the true poets are, therefore, ministers of the soul. And all who minister to the soul are poets, for each exposes the shape and substance of being and becoming divine. It is my unfailing perception that in no other instance is the foregoing observation more applicable than to the author of this very enlightened literary achievement. I am blessed to have been an acquaintance for more than thirty years."

—*Raymond J. Jackson, EEO Director (Retired), National Institutes of Health*

*   *   *

"Growing up in the north, I did not get a chance to experience the civil rights movement. After moving to the south years later, I only witnessed the civil rights struggle by way of television. **From the Back of the Line** will allow me to share thoughts of the civil rights movement with my children and my grandchildren."

—*Mrs. Dianne Evans, Church Musician, Atlanta, GA.*

"This book is a good idea because education is liberation. It will help our youth absolutely. They will learn to move from the back of the line and assume a position of leadership at the forefront of leadership positions in our communities."

—*The Honorable Tyrone Brooks, President, Georgia Association of Black Elected Officials and State Representative, District 63*

ACKNOWLEDGMENTS

"I give God the Glory" for the things that God has done for me, in me, and through me, in completing this long overdue book, *From the Back of the Line*.

Much gratitude I give to all who have assisted me, in any manner, with this project. Without the prayers and the words of encouragement from my friends and family, this project would not have been completed.

I want to pay a special memorial tribute to my loving parents, William H. Ward, Sr. and Mrs. Mary L. Ward for allowing me to see the light of day in Albany, Georgia. I offer a spirit of thanksgiving to my husband Daniel W. Wright, Jr., who has assisted me in creative ways in preparation for the release of this book. I offer a debt of gratitude to my son, Byron Ward Wright, a "marketing whiz" who has a great future ahead of him and to my step-daughter, Angeleque, her husband, Louis Jenkins, to Jamile, Kendra, and Baby Kendra for just being you. Thanks to Markus and Sandy Sanders for their calls and best wishes . . . special thanks to my spiritual daughter, Keaver Brenai, for your prayers, your support, and your computer expertise, to my administrative assistant R. Pamela Adams for assisting me in marketing this project, for business cards, and a great website, to Chalayia Rivers and Bobby L. Carter for your prayers and your assistance, and to Minister Bruce Sutchar, Richard Innocent, Dr. Ann Smith, A. E. Jenkins, the *Atlanta Journal Constitution Gwinnett*, and the *Gwinnett Daily Post* newspapers, and to Ike Washington for your encouragement and beautiful contributions of photography. To Janssen Robinson, for the beautiful way that you sketched my vision for the book cover, to Mary Royal Jenkins, and to Rev. Dr. Merchuria Chase Williams and Jewel Biggs for your editorial comments, to Rev. Dr. N'dugu G.B. T' Ofori-atta for your wisdom and your encouragement, and to Charlie Wright (not related, but supportive, indeed) for repairing three computers for me during this project.

I also express my thanks to Amy Holland for being a dedicated prayer warrior for me and for this project, to my extended family, Tommy and Yoshiko Toyomura for your love and support, to my senior citizen friends, to all the missionaries—worldwide, to my co-laborers and prayer partners in the Lord, especially Dianne Evans, Sherma Owens, Rev. Dr. Jeannette Holt, Rev. Margrite Roberts, Rev. Dr. Margaret Richardson, Rev. Dr. Arthur L. Hilson, and to Archbishop Moses and Bishop Margie de la Rosa, to my friend, Raymond J. Jackson who gave me the referral for my publisher and to Attorney William Nelson Martin for writing the *Preface* and for his wisdom and support, to my former student Valerie Boyd who inspired me to make this book a reality, and to Alvelyn Sanders who gave me wise counsel, and to Kay Smith Pedrotti who wrote the *Foreword* and offered me editorial advice, to my very dear friends in the ministry, to Bishop and Mrs. Clarence Carr and to the Episcopal fathers of the African Methodist Episcopal Zion Church (AME Zion), to the ministers of all ranks, to the missionary supervisors, to the presiding elders, and the members and friends of the "Freedom Church," and especially to my dedicated congregation, Simmons Chapel A.M.E. Zion Church.

I thank Rev. Emmanuel T. Solo, my very dedicated associate minister, and members of the Atlanta Family Church and Faith A.M.E. Zion Church. I give special thanks to the officers and members of the Concerned Black Clergy of Atlanta, Inc., to the officers, members, and especially the ministers of the American Clergy Leadership Conference and to the Inter-religious International Federation for World Peace and to the members of the United Nations, to the Ambassadors of Peace, and to the members of organizations that promote peace and reconciliation.

I thank God for my special friends, ministers, imams, and rabbis whom I have met from all over the world, including members of the March Prayer Breakfast Club and the Red Hat Society, I give God praise for your love, for your friendship, for your support, and for your prayers. Many of my friends and supporters have remained faithful to me, over the years, from my hometown of Albany, Georgia, to Bandera, Texas; from North Carolina to Mount Vernon, New York; from Lawrenceville to London, from Israel to Canada, and from the four corners of the world—I thank you.

I greatly appreciate the assistance of TaxConcepts LLC and the assistance of attorney and author, Michele Clark-Jenkins who gave me sound advice and suggestions about publishing this book. I extend my heartfelt special thanks to Martha Jablow who, indeed, was a Godsend. She pushed me to complete this project with her support and editorial services, and thanks to publishing consultant Mary Jervis and to the staff at Xlibris Corporation.

Last but not least, I thank God for the blessings and prayers of my siblings, Barbara W. Carroll, William H. Ward, Jr., Ernest J. Ward, Carl F. Ward, Ella J. Ward, and Cassandra D. Ward. I thank God for my aunts, my uncles, my nieces, my nephews, my cousins, and to my God-daughters Brandi Ray and Angela Byrd, and again, To God Be the Glory!!!